Software Engineering: Specification, Implementation, Verification

Suad Alagić

Software Engineering: Specification, Implementation, Verification

 Springer

Suad Alagić
Portland, Maine, USA

ISBN 978-3-319-87099-1   ISBN 978-3-319-61518-9   (eBook)
DOI 10.1007/978-3-319-61518-9

Printed on acid-free paper

This Springer imprint is published by Springer Nature
The registered company is Springer International Publishing AG
The registered company address is: Gewerbestrasse 11, 6330 Cham, Switzerland

For
Adrian, Evan, Lucas, and Dario.

Preface

This book is based on my experiences in teaching Software Engineering courses. It is meant to be a textbook for an upper level undergraduate course on Software Engineering, and perhaps for first year graduate courses. This book differs significantly from the existing textbooks on Software Engineering in several fundamental ways. A major distinction is the use of constraints in all phases of software development. The existing books on Software Engineering are mostly on analysis, design, documentation, software project management and related issues and not on the software itself. Because of that many recent developments in software technologies that are critical for software engineering are missing from those texts. Technical coverage of data management issues and software verification are two further major distinctive properties of this book.

Analysis and design are in the existing books on Software Engineering typically presented using UML diagrams. However, a major component of the UML Standard is OCL (Object Constraint Language). Specification of constraints in a language such as OCL is very limited in the existing texts on Software Engineering if it is present at all. UML diagrams are simply insufficient for specification of the designed model. The UML diagrams are subject to different interpretations by the implementors. Usage of a constraint language such as OCL produces a much more precise specification of the designed model. These specifications are in fact the requirements for the implementors to produce code that indeed satisfies the specifications. In addition, such an approach leads to the usage of software verification techniques that have been developed recently.

The technical details that are needed in order to implement the designed model using object-oriented programming languages are typically missing in the existing textbooks on Software Engineering. This is why these texts have very little material on the actual software. Subtle issues related to the usage of parametric types to represent associations in the UML models, subtleties of the interplay of inheritance and subtyping, the impact of dynamic binding in forward and reverse engineering, refactoring and model and code transformations are thus not presented at the required technical level. The role of interfaces in mapping models to code is neglected, perhaps because the interfaces are given a side role in UML models. This leads to poor management of the levels of abstraction, which is critical in software development.

In most applications, data management is a critical issue. Data management requires specialized models and software technologies. Without a correct solution for data management a software project is bound to failure. In spite of that software engineering issues when it comes to data management have very limited coverage in the existing books on software engineering. The technical level of those presentations is not even close to what database and related technologies have to offer. In this book, data management is given the attention that it requires in order to make a software project a success. A related issue is that use cases should typically be implemented as transactions. Transaction technologies are completely missing from the existing texts on software engineering. In this book, those technologies have the place that they deserve.

Lack of coverage of OCL as a major component of the UML Standard leads to multiple implications. The absence of specifications makes it impossible to verify that the produced code actually has the required properties. OCL is not the only object-oriented specification language available. There are several object-oriented specification languages that are tied to particular object-oriented programming languages. In these technologies code is annotated with specifications so that it can be verified that the code actually satisfies the specifications. This is done preferably statically using a verifying compiler or more commonly constraints are enforced at run-time and violations are then handled. Since static verification is obviously preferable, there are several open-source projects offering static verification. None of this is in the existing textbooks on Software Engineering. For the first time we give a detailed presentation of the usage of OCL to document models based on UML. We also elaborate how specifications are used in a particular implementation language so that they are subject to dynamic or static verification.

Portland, Maine, USA   Suad Alagić
Spring 2017

Acknowledgements

The author is grateful to two software engineers, Russell Gillen and Thomas Keschl, his former graduate students, for their numerous valuable comments that significantly improved the manuscript.

Contents

About the Author

Suad Alagić holds a PhD in Computer Science from the University of Massachusetts at Amherst. He has been Computer Science Professor at multiple universities for many years. His research areas are Object-Oriented Software Systems, Database Systems, and Programming Languages and Systems. Suad Alagić previously published four books with Springer. His first book on assertions was translated into Japanese, Russian and Polish. Suad Alagić is the lead author of numerous papers that were published in the proceedings of highly visible conferences and in prestigious journals. The most important publications are at

http://dblp.uni-trier.de/pers/hd/a/Alagic:Suad

Suad Alagić had research grants from NSF and DOD and was an invited staff member of ODMG. Suad Alagić held visiting research positions at Microsoft Research and University of Tokyo. His extensive teaching experience includes a variety of object-oriented courses.

Chapter 1
Analysis and Design

The starting point of system analysis is an application environment consisting of different types of users and different activities that they are involved in. The users in the application environment that initiate and carry out activities in that environment are called actors. The activities and hence their actors have information requirements that are necessary in order to perform those activities. The task of system analysis is specification of different types of users, their activities, and the requirements that those activities have in order to perform correctly their task.

The task of the system design is to produce a specification of a technical system that supports the activities specified in the analysis phase in such a way that the requirements for those activities are satisfied. The result of a system design is a model of an application environment that is suitable for implementation using an appropriate software technology.

A model of an application environment is an abstraction that specifies only the relevant features of that environment as determined by the activities to be supported in the newly designed system. Such a model is specified using a well-defined modeling framework. A modeling framework must be able to specify different types of entities in the application environment, actors in particular. In addition, the modeling framework should be able to represent relationships that exist between different entities in the application environment. Most importantly, a modeling framework must be able to specify the activities in the application environment as triggered by actors. These activities become use cases for the newly designed system, i.e., they represent different ways of using the system.

The level of abstraction of the model designed in the system analysis should be such that the model is independent of a particular implementation. This way the model may be redesigned to reflect the changes in its application environment that happen over time. At the same time, the model must be implementable using an available software technology.

© Springer International Publishing AG 2017
S. Alagić, *Software Engineering: Specification, Implementation, Verification*,
DOI 10.1007/978-3-319-61518-9_1

In this chapter we consider several application environments. For each one of them we specify different types of relevant entities and their relationships. We specify the most important use cases and their requirements. All of this is done using our view of the UML modeling framework in ways that is not typical in the existing literature, as explained in the preface of this book.

1.1   Specification of Use Cases

Consider first an investment management application. We identify two groups of users of respective types *Investor* and *Broker*. Investors and brokers are called actors in the UML terminology because they invoke actions in the investment management system.

These actions may be clustered into two groups shown in Fig. 1.1.The two groups of use cases are *Investing* and *OverseeingPortfolios* and they may be viewed as subsystems of the overall system.

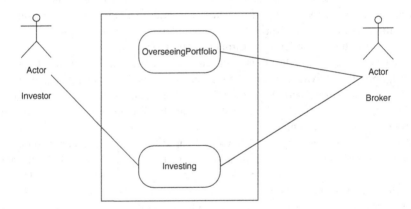

Fig. 1.1   Investment management

The investing use cases are displaying a portfolio, buying an asset, and selling an asset. The overseeing use cases are displaying a portfolio, displaying available assets, and approving a transaction that an investor required by selling or buying assets. These use cases are specified in Fig. 1.2.

In order to specify a use case we first specify entities involved in a use case. Consider the use cases *BuyAsset* and *SellAsset*. An investor selects an asset, asks for approval of his broker, and if approved he completes the transaction so that the purchased asset now appears in the investor's portfolio. So the entities involved in these use cases are of type *Investor, Asset, Portfolio* and *Broker*.

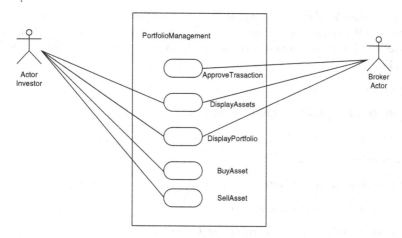

Fig. 1.2   Portfolio management use cases

The next step in specification of a use case is specification of conditions under which the use case may be invoked. These conditions are called preconditions. The outcome of invocation of a use case is specified by its postconditions. The preconditions for the use case *BuyAsset* are that the asset price is acceptable and that the broker approves the transaction. The effect of a use case is specified in its postconditions that are required to hold in the system after the use case is completed. The postcondition of the use case *BuyAsset* is that the asset is in the portfolio.

In addition to the pre- and postconditions, full specification of a use case also includes specification of the impact of invoking a use case on entities that are not specified in these constraints. A particularly important aspect is the impact on other constraints that the system should satisfy. This is expressed by frame constraints. The frame constraints for the use cases *BuyAsset* and *SellAsset* specify that all the other assets in the portfolio will be unaffected by invocation of these use cases.

Use case: BuyAsset

Entities: Investor, Asset, Portfolio, Broker

Actors: Investor, Broker

Constraints:

Preconditions: assetPriceOK, brokerApproves

Postconditions: assetInPortfolio

Frame: All other assets in portfolio unaffected

The use case *SellAsset* is symmetric. The preconditions are that the asset is in the portfolio of the investor who initiated the use case and that the broker approves the transaction. The postcondition ensures that the asset is no longer in the investor's portfolio.

Use case: SellAsset

Entities: Investor, Asset, Portfolio, Broker

Actors: Investor, Broker

Constraints:

Preconditions: assetInPortfolio, brokerApproves

Postconditions: not assetInPortfolio

Frame: All other assets in portfolio unaffected

Statements such as *assetPriceOK*, *brokerApproves*, *assetInPortfolio*, not *assetInPortfolio* etc. are informally specified predicates that evaluate to true or false. All these specifications will be expressed in Chap. 2 in a language associated with UML called Object Constraint Language (OCL).

Consider now a more complex flight management application. The flight management application has two types of actors: *Scheduler* and *Passenger*. Use cases of this system are partitioned into two groups: *Scheduling* and *Reservations* as shown in Fig. 1.3.

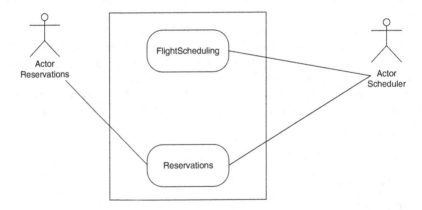

Fig. 1.3 Flight management

Scheduling consists of use cases *DisplayFlights*, *ScheduleFlight*, *RedirectFlight*, and *CancelFlight*. Reservations consists of use cases *DisplayFlights*, *MakeReservation*, and *DeleteReservation*. These use cases are shown in Fig. 1.4.

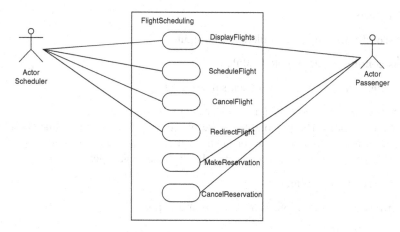

Fig. 1.4 Flight management use cases

The entities involved in *ScheduleFlight* use case are *Scheduler*, *FlightSchedule*, *Flight*, *Aircraft*, and *Airport*. The preconditions for invoking this use case are that the flight is not already scheduled, that the origin and the destination airports are available, and that an aircraft is available. The postcondition ensures that the flight is in the flight schedule. The frame constraint ensures that scheduling a flight does not affect other scheduled flights.

Use case: ScheduleFlight

Entities: Scheduler, FlightSchedule, Flight, Aircraft, Airport

Actors: Scheduler

Constraints:

Preconditions: not flightScheduled, originAirportAvailable, destinationAirportAvailable, aircraftAvailable

Postconditions: flightScheduled

Frame: All other scheduled flights unaffected

The entities involved in the use case *CancelFlight* are *Scheduler*, *FlightSchedule* and *Flight*. The preconditions are that the flight is scheduled and that its status is not *inflight*. The postcondition is that the flight is not scheduled any more.

Use case: CancelFlight

Entities: Scheduler, FlightSchedule, Flight

Actors: Scheduler

Constraints:

Preconditions: flightScheduled, not inFlight

Postconditions: not flightScheduled

Frame: Schedule of all other flights unaffected

The use case *RedirectFlight* involves entities of types *Scheduler*, *FlightSchedule*, *Flight* and *Airport*. The preconditions are that the flight is in flight, that the new destination is different from the original destination, and that the new airport is available. The postcondition ensures that the flight has a new destination.

Use case: RedirectFlight

Entities: Scheduler, FlightSchedule, Flight, Airport

Actors: Scheduler

Constraints:

Preconditions: inFlight, newDestination notEqual destination, newAirportAvailable

Postconditions: destination equal newDestination

Frame: flightScheduled, schedule of all other flights unaffected

The use case *MakeReservation* involves an actor of type *Passenger*. The other entity in this use case is *FlightSchedule*. The precondition is that the desired flight is available and the postcondition is that the reservation is confirmed. The frame constraint guarantees that this use case does not affect any other reservation.

Use case: MakeReservation

Constraints:

Entities: Passenger, FlightSchedule

Actors: Passenger

Preconditions: flightAvailable

Postconditions: reservationConfirmed

Frame: Other reservations not affected

The use case *CancelReservation* involves the same entity types as *MakeReservation*. The precondition is that the reservation is confirmed and the postcondition that the reservation is not confirmed.

Use case: CancelReservation

Entities: Passenger, FlightSchedule

Actors: Passenger

Constraints:

Preconditions: reservationConfirmed

Postconditions: not reservationConfirmed

Frame: Other reservations not affected

1.2 Structural Modeling

In addition to specification of entities involved in a use case, we also specify their relationships. UML modeling philosophy includes two types of relationships among entities in the modelled application environment: associations and inheritance. We consider associations first. These are particular constraints that hold in the application environment of the system. In the investment management application, an investor is associated with a single portfolio and a portfolio has a unique owner. The association between an investor and portfolio is thus one to one. A broker manages multiple portfolios, and a portfolio has a unique broker so the association of a broker and its portfolios is one to many. A portfolio includes multiple assets and an asset appears in multiple portfolios, hence this association is many to many. These associations reflect the semantics of the application environment and could be different from the above specifications. The relationships among entities in this application are specified in Fig. 1.5. Each association is equipped with multiplicity indicators as discussed above. 0..* stands for zero or more occurrences.

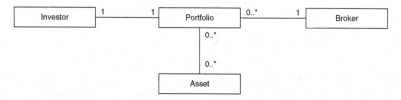

Fig. 1.5 Investment management associations

Associations were described above as they apply to this particular application. However, it is the inheritance relationships that are in the core of the object-oriented paradigm. Figure 1.6 shows that in this particular application inheritance is the required modeling technique. In Fig. 1.6 there is a generic entity *Asset*, with two subtypes, *Stock* and *Bond*. These two subtypes inherit all the properties of the generic type *Asset* and in addition feature some specific properties that apply to the subtypes and not to the generic type.

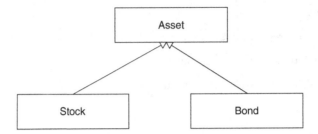

Fig. 1.6 Asset inheritance hierarchy

A diagram that represents the association and the inheritance relationships in this application is given in Fig. 1.7. In this diagram end points of associations are named which allows traversal of these relationships to be used extensively in Chap. 2.

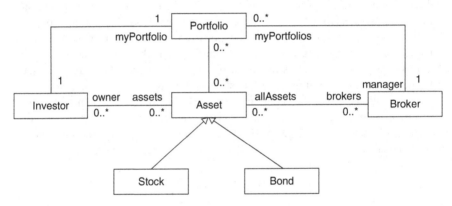

Fig. 1.7 Portfolio management associations and inheritance

The inheritance relationships in the flight scheduling model are represented in Figs. 1.8 and 1.9. The structural model of this application specifies two subtypes of the entity type *Flight* (*DomesticFlight* and *InternationalFlight*) and two subtypes of the entity type *Airport* (*DomesticAirport* and *InternationalAirport*).

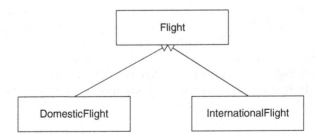

Fig. 1.8 Inheritance in flight scheduling

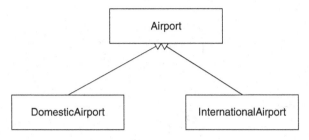

Fig. 1.9   Airport inheritance hierarchy

Consider now the entity types and their associations in the flight management application. A flight schedule is associated with a collection of flights, a collection of aircraft, and a collection of airports (at least two). On the other hand, a flight is associated with a single flight schedule, and so is each aircraft and each airport.

The entity types and their relationships in the flight management application are given in Fig. 1.10 in which the end points of associations are named. This makes it possible to access all flights, all airports, and all aircraft in a flight schedule. These relationships are bidirectional in the UML terminology. Specifically, this means that given a flight, it is possible to access the flight schedule to which it belongs, and likewise for aircraft and airports.

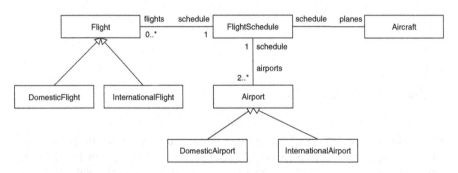

Fig. 1.10   Flight scheduling associations and inheritance

1.3   Behavioral Specifications: Sequence Diagrams

It is critical to understand that the specifications that we considered so far are entirely declarative. They do not say anything about a sequence of actions that is needed in order to satisfy the constraints associated with a use case. In the

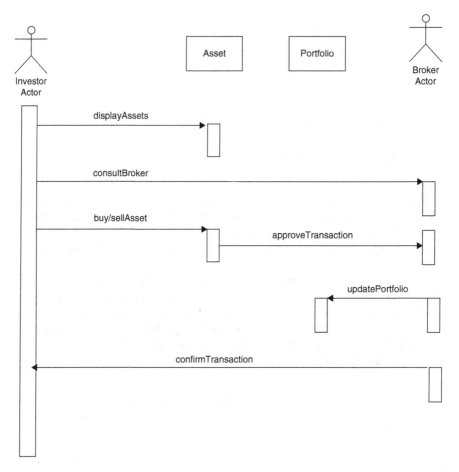

Fig. 1.11 Investment sequence diagram

UML style these sequences of actions are represented by sequence diagrams. The sequence diagram for the use cases *BuyAsset/SellAsset* is given in Fig. 1.11. It contains entities involved in the use case specified along the horizontal axis, time represented by the vertical axis oriented downward, and the messages sent and received by the involved entities as they happen in time.

The sequence diagram for the *ScheduleFlight* use case is represented in Fig. 1.12.

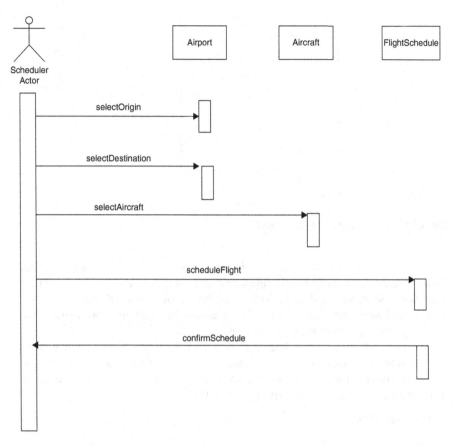

Fig. 1.12   Flight scheduling sequence diagram

1.4   Putting It All Together: Use Cases, Entity Diagrams and Sequence Diagrams

We will illustrate the analysis techniques discussed so far in a particular application. In the course management application, we can identify two groups of users of respective types *Student* and *Registrar*. Students and registrars are actors in the course management system.

The actions may be clustered into two groups. The first group is called *Scheduling* and consists of course scheduling actions. The other group of use cases is called *Enrollment* and it deals with enrollment into courses. We can view these two groups of use cases as subsystems of the overall system. The registrar actor interacts with both of these two subsystems and the student actor interacts only with the subsystem that handles course enrollment (Fig. 1.13).

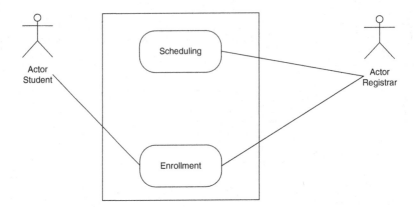

Fig. 1.13 Course management application

Two main use cases in the *Scheduling* subsystem are *ScheduleCourse* and *DeleteCourse*. In order to specify these two use cases we first specify the entities that those use cases involve. In both cases the entities involved are of the types *Course* and *Registrar*. We also specify the actors for every use case, which is of type *Registrar* in both of these two use cases.

The preconditions for the *ScheduleCourse* use case are that the course is not already scheduled, that an instructor is available, and that a classroom is available. The postcondition for the use case *ScheduleCourse* is that the course is scheduled. The use case *SchedueCourse* is specified as follows:

Use case: ScheduleCourse

Entities: Course, Registrar

Actors: Registrar

Constraints:

Preconditions: not courseScheduled, instructorAvailable, classroomAvailable

Postconditions: courseScheduled

Frame: Schedule of all other courses unaffected

The precondition for the use case *DeleteCourse* is that the course is actually in the schedule. The postcondition of the use case *DeleteCourse* is that the course is not scheduled any more. In the use cases *ScheduleCourse* and *DeleteCourse*, the frame constraints specify that other courses are not affected by these use cases.

Use case: DeleteCourse

Entities: Course, Registrar

Actors: Registrar

Constraints:

Preconditions: courseScheduled

Postconditions: not courseScheduled

Frame: All other scheduled courses unaffected

Consider now the relationships among entity types of the course management application. A registrar is associated with a number of instructors and an instructor with a single registrar. A registrar is associated with a number of courses and so is an instructor. On the other hand, a course is associated with a single registrar and a single instructor. These associations are shown in Fig. 1.14. They reflect the semantics of the application environment and could be different from the above specifications.

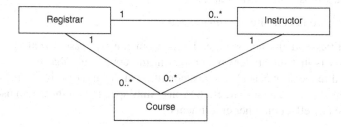

Fig. 1.14 Associations for ScheduleCourse use case

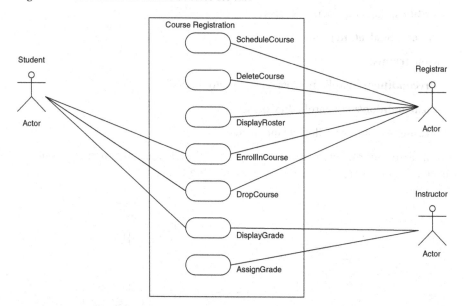

Fig. 1.15 Course registration use cases

The most important use cases in the *Enrollment* subsystem are *EnrollInCourse* and *DropCourse*. The entities involved in *EnrollInCourse* are of types *Student*, *Course*, and *Registrar*. The actors are of type *Student*. The preconditions are that the course is open and that the student who initiated this use case satisfies the prerequisites for the course. The postcondition is that the student is enrolled in the course.

Use case: EnrollInCourse

Entities: Student, Course, Registrar

Actors: Student, Registrar

Constraints:

Preconditions: courseOpen, prerequisitesSatisfied

Postconditions: enrolledInCourse

Frame: All other enrollments unaffected

The entities and the actions are the same in the use case *DropCourse*. The precondition is that the student is enrolled in the course and that the use case is invoked within the drop period. The postcondition of this use case is that the student is not enrolled in the course. The frame constraints specify that these two use cases do not have any effect on other enrollments.

Use case: DropCourse

Entities: Student, Course, Registrar

Actors: Student, Registrar

Constraints:

Preconditions: enrolledInCourse,withinDropPeriod

Postconditions: not enrolledInCourse

Frame: All other enrollments unaffected

The association diagram in Fig. 1.16 specifies the relationships among the entities involved in the use cases *EnrollInCourse* and *DropCourse*.

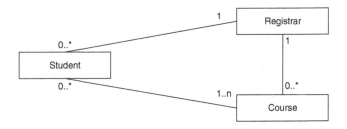

Fig. 1.16 Enroll in course association diagram

Unlike these specifications that are entirely declarative, in the UML style sequences of actions needed to implement a use case are represented by sequence diagrams. The sequence diagram for the use case *DropCourse* is given in Fig. 1.17.

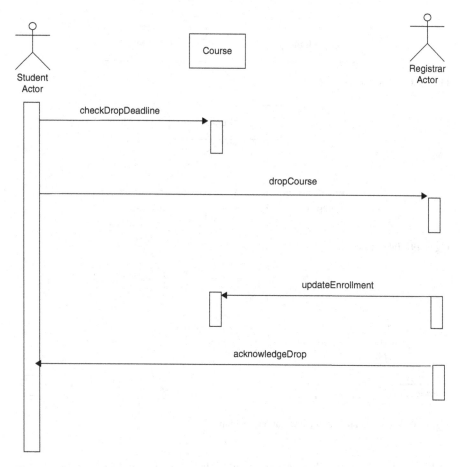

Fig. 1.17 Drop course sequence diagram

Figures 1.18 and 1.19 contain two situations in this particular application in which inheritance is the required modeling technique. In Fig. 1.18 there is a generic entity type *Student*, with two subtypes, *Undergraduate* and *Graduate*. The entity type *Student* contains generic properties that apply to all students. The two subtypes inherit all those properties of the generic type *Student* and in addition have some specific properties that apply to the subtypes and not to the generic type.

Another case of inheritance is given in Fig. 1.19 which contains one generic entity type *Instructor* with two subtypes *Lecturer* and *Professor*.

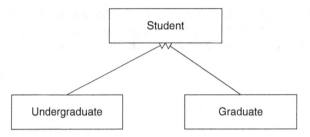

Fig. 1.18   Inheritance

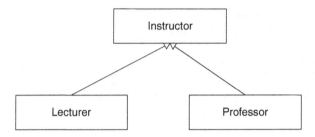

Fig. 1.19   Inheritance

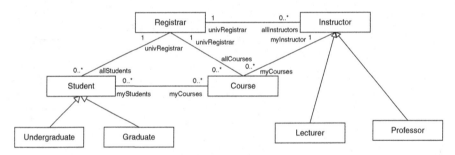

Fig. 1.20   Course management associations and inheritance

Figure 1.20 specifies the association and inheritance relationships in the course management system.

1.5   Aggregation

Aggregation is a particular form of association between entity types that allows specification of a complex entity type in terms of entity types that represent its components. For example, in Fig. 1.21 an entity type *Schedule* is defined as an aggregate of entity types *Course*, *Student* and *Instructor*.

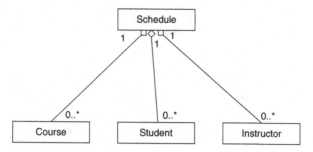

Fig. 1.21 Course schedule as an aggregate entity type

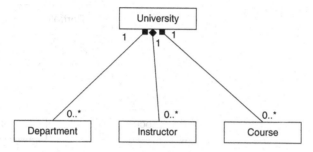

Fig. 1.22 University as an aggregate entity type

A stronger form of aggregation is specified in Fig. 1.22. The entity type *University* is defined as an aggregate of the entity types *Department, Instructor* and *Course*. In the type of aggregation specified in Fig. 1.21 instances of the component types can exist independently of the instance of the entity type *Schedule*. In the form of aggregation specified in Fig. 1.22 components cannot exist independently of an instance of the type *University*. Deleting an instance of the type *Schedule* does not cause deletion of its component courses, instructors or students. Deleting an instance of the type *University* causes deletion of its associated components representing departments, courses and instructors.

Another example of strong aggregation given in Fig. 1.23 is the entity type *InvestmentBank*. Components of an instance of this type are assets, portfolios and brokers. These component instances cannot exist if their associated investment bank instance does not exist. An investment bank instance owns its components, and if an investment bank instance is deleted, so are its components.

The entity type *Portfolio* is defined in Fig. 1.24 as a weak aggregation of the entity types *Stock* and *Bond*. This means that if a portfolio is deleted, stocks and bond instances that are components of the portfolio will continue to exist.

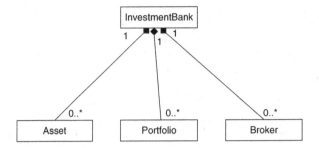

Fig. 1.23 Investment bank as an aggregate entity type

Fig. 1.24 Portfolio as an
aggregate entity type

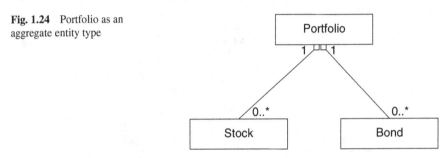

1.6 Entity Types as Interfaces

The first step in our methodology in specifying entity types is to view them as UML interfaces. An interface of an entity type specifies signatures of operations or actions applicable to instances of that type. So it is in fact a communication interface for instances of that type specifying what kind of messages such instances are able to send and receive. A signature of an operation of an interface consists of the name of the operation, the types of its arguments, and the type of the result of the operation. When an operation is an action that produces no specific result, the result type is omitted. This is the case with actions *buyAsset* and *sellAsset* of the interface *Investor* specified in Fig. 1.25. Operations *getPortfolio* and *getBroker* reflect the one to one relationships between an investor and its portfolio and its broker. The symbol + indicates that all of the operations of an interface are public.

Fig. 1.25 Investor interface

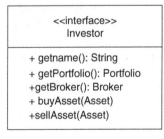

The operations *getPortfolios* of the interface *Asset* specified in Fig. 1.26 reflect a many to many relationship between assets and portfolios in which those assets appear.

Fig. 1.26   Asset interface

<<interface>> Asset
+ getAssetId(): String +getValue(): float +getPortfolios: CollectionOfPortfolios

The operations *getOwner* and *getBroker* of the interface *Portfolio* specified in Fig. 1.27 reflect one to one association between a portfolio and its owner and between a portfolio and its broker. The operation *getAssets* produces the collection of all assets of a portfolio reflecting many to many association between portfolios and assets.

Fig. 1.27   Portfolio interface

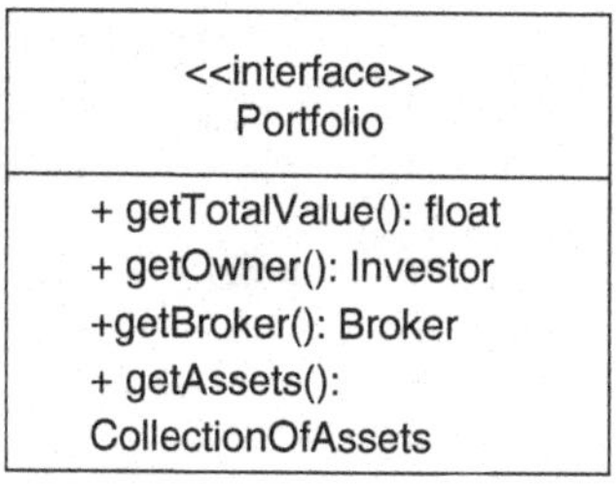

<<interface>> Portfolio
+ getTotalValue(): float + getOwner(): Investor +getBroker(): Broker + getAssets(): CollectionOfAssets

The operation *getAllAssets* of the interface *Broker* specified in Fig. 1.28 produces a collection of all assets. This reflects a many to many association between brokers and assets. The operation *getMyPortfolios* is a reflection of the one to many association between brokers and portfolios that they manage.

Fig. 1.28   Broker interface

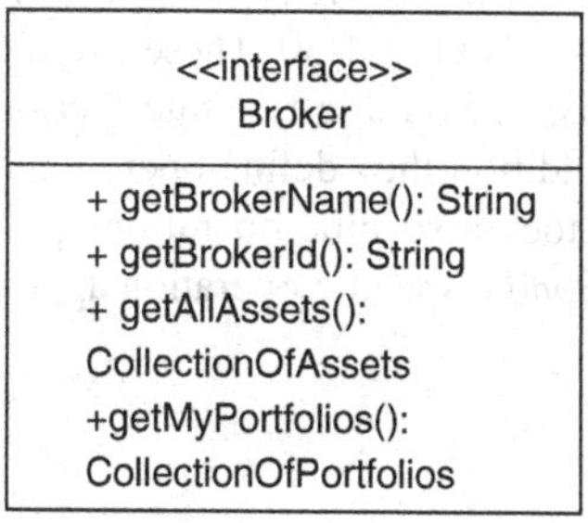

<<interface>> Broker
+ getBrokerName(): String + getBrokerId(): String + getAllAssets(): CollectionOfAssets +getMyPortfolios(): CollectionOfPortfolios

Fig. 1.29 Stock interface

Fig. 1.30 Bond interface

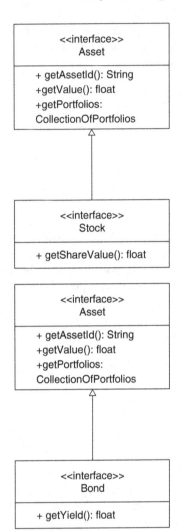

Two specific types of assets are represented by interfaces *Stock* in Fig. 1.29 and *Bond* in Fig. 1.30. These two interfaces are derived by inheritance from the interface *Asset*. So these two interfaces inherit all the operations applicable to assets and in addition they define operations applicable to these two subtypes. For the interface Stock a specific operation applicable to stocks is *getShareValue*. For the interface *Bond* a specific operation applicable to bonds is *getYield*.

1.7   Entity Types as Classes

The next step in specifying entity types is to define them as UML classes. A UML class of an entity type specifies the components of state of instances of that entity type. These components are called attributes or fields. So a class associated with an interface specifies some of the implementation aspects of that interface. This is why a class is said to realize or implement its interfaces. However, unlike a class in an object-oriented programming language, a UML class does not specify implementation of operations. It just specifies their signatures like interfaces do.

In the class *Investor* given in Fig. 1.31 components of the state of instances of this entity type are name, broker and portfolio. Specification of an attribute consists of its name and its type. The minus signs indicates that these attributes are private for the entity type *Investor*, i.e., inaccessible to other entity types. The operations of this class are specified as public in the interface of this class. A class can have operations that are not defined in its interfaces, and they might be declared private or public.

Fig. 1.31   Investor class

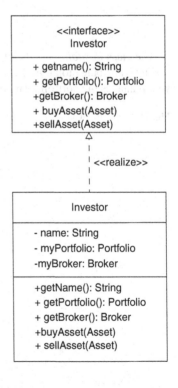

Figure 1.32 specifies a UML class *Asset* and its interface. The components of the state of an instance of the entity type *Asset* are asset identifier and its value.

Fig. 1.32 Asset class

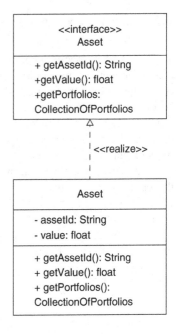

The class *Portfolio* and its interface are specified in Fig. 1.33. This specification includes attributes total value, the investor who is the portfolio owner, the broker who manages the portfolio, and the collections of stocks and bonds in the portfolio.

Fig. 1.33 PortfolioClass

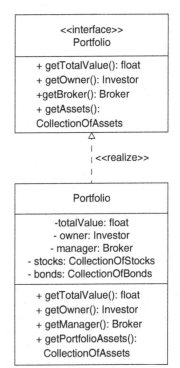

The class *Broker* specified in Fig. 1.34 has attributes broker identifier and broker name.

Fig. 1.34   Broker class

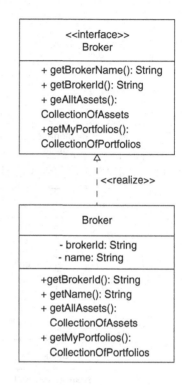

Consider now the class *Stock* specified in Fig. 1.35. This class implements the interface *Stock* and specifies an attribute *shareValue*. The interface *Stock* inherits from the interface *Asset*. The class *Asset* implements the interface *Asset*. The class *Stock* inherits from the class *Asset*. This determines the fields and operations of the class *Stock*. The attributes are *assetId*, *value*, and *shareValue*. The operations are *getAssetId*, *getValue*, *getPortfolios*, and *getShareValue*. This situation is called diamond inheritance. It includes multiple inheritance in which the class *Stock* implements its interface *Stock* and inherits from the class *Asset*. The general rule is that multiple inheritance may be applied to interfaces and single inheritance to classes. This will be discussed in more detail in Chap. 3. A similar situation occurs for the class *Bond*.

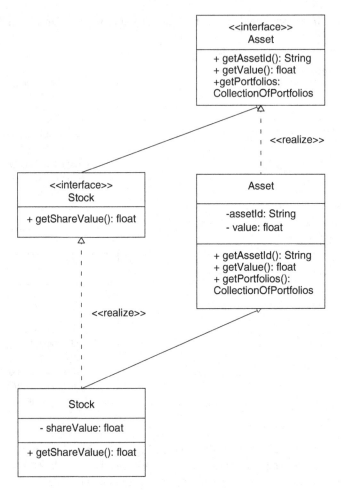

Fig. 1.35 Classes and interfaces

1.8 Exercises

1. Specify use cases (such as *ApproveTransaction*) of the *OverseeingPortfolio* subsystem of the Investment management application.
2. Specify use cases *BuyStock* and *SellStock* and likewise *BuyBond* and *SellBond* of the Investment management application. Specify the relationship of these use cases with the use cases *BuyAsset* and *SellAsset*.
3. Specify sequence diagrams for use cases *CancelFlight* and *RedirectFlight* of the Flight management application.
4. Specify sequence diagrams for the use cases *MakeReservation* and *Cancel-Reservation* of the Flight management application.

5. Specify sequence diagrams for use cases *ScheduleCourse*, *DeleteCourse* and *EnrollInCourse* of the Course management application.
6. For the model of an investment bank in Figs. 1.23 and 1.24 specify use cases *EstablishBank* and *DissolveBank*.
7. For the model of an investment bank in Figs. 1.23 and 1.24 specify use cases *EstablishPortfolio* and *DeletePortfolio*.
8. For the Course management application specify in the UML style the interface *Registrar* and its associated class.
9. For the Course management application specify in the UML style the interface *Student* and its associated class.
10. For the Course management application specify in the UML style the interface *Course* and its associated class.

Chapter 2
Specification of Constraints

Behavior of objects of a class is specified in UML by signatures of methods of that class. These signatures specify what kind of messages an object can send to other objects or receive from them. However, a UML class does not contain specifications of the actual behavior of objects of that class, i.e., what happens when an object sends or receives a message. Some behavioral properties are specified in the associated diagrams that attempt to specify some aspects of behavior. We discussed sequence diagrams, which specify a sequence of actions in a use case as they happen in time. However, that is still far from specifying precisely behavior of objects of a class. This behavior is specified in associated constraint language OCL (Object Constraint Language) which is the topic of this chapter.

Although OCL is a part of the UML standard, its usage in the specification of the design is not typical. The thrust of this book is that the specification of constraints is critical. Not only do these specifications complete documentation of the result of the design, they also specify the requirements for the code to be produced after the design is completed.

OCL is a declarative, specification language and as such it does not deal with details of the programming language representation of a class. It specifies in a declarative fashion behavior of entities in an application environment. These specifications are given at a much higher level of abstraction than the level of programming languages.

2.1 Class Invariants

Our presentation of OCL is based on the following sample of UML classes and their associations given in Fig. 2.1.

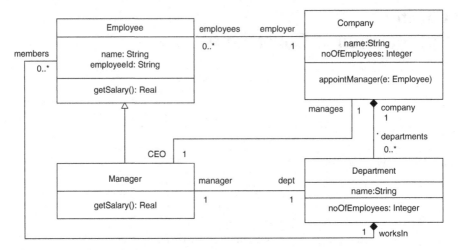

Fig. 2.1 Company class diagram

Properties of all objects of a class are specified in class invariants. A class invariant specifies the context to which it applies by providing the class name. A reference to an object of a class is specified using the keyword *self*. References to attributes are specified using the dot notation. For example, *self.noOfEmployees* in a class *Company* refers to the number of employees of a particular company denoted by *self*. The invariant properties of objects of a class are specified by expressions that are called constraints.

For example, the type of an attribute *noOfEmployees* is specified as integer in the UML class   *Company*, but the actual range of values by a constraint *self.noOfEmplyees >=0*. This particular invariant has the following specification in OCL:

context Company **inv**:
  self.noOfEmplyees >= 0

Class invariants can refer to methods as in the example below which contains invocation of a method *getSalary*.

context Employee **inv**:
  self.getSalary()>= 10,000

More complex invariants may be defined using logical operators as in the following example:

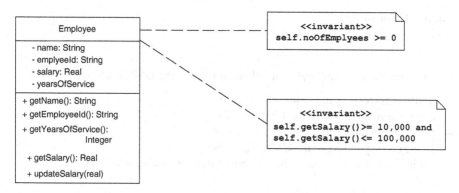

Fig. 2.2 Invariant of class Employee

context Employee **inv**:
  self.getSalary()>= 10,000 **and**
  self.getSalary()<= 100,000

An invariant is represented in a UML diagram as a note shown in Fig. 2.2. This diagram contains a more elaborate representation of the class *Employee*.

Dot notation is also used in OCL to traverse relationships. For example, CEO is a 1:1 relationship between entity types *Company* and *Manager*. An example of a constraint that specifies that a manager of a company has salary greater than $100,000 is specified as follows:

context Company **inv**:
  self.CEO.getSalary() >= 100,000

Traversing a relationship between a company and its employees is specified in the class invariant given below. This invariant specifies that the number of employees computed by traversing the relationship *employees* of a company must be the same as the number of employees of the company. This case is an example of a reference to a method *count* that applies to a collection of objects and is denoted by the symbol − >.

context Company **inv**:
  self.employees− > count() = self.noOfEmployees

A similar example that specifies traversal of the relationship *employees* and contains application of the function *notempty* to the collection of employees is given below. *notempty* is a boolean function that tests whether the collection to which it is applied is nonempty. Since this operator applies to a collection, its application is denoted by the symbol − >.

context Company **inv**:
 self.employees − > notempty()

OCL predefined simple types and their corresponding UML types are:

− *Boolean* corresponding to the UML type *boolean.*
− *Integer* corresponding to the UML type *integer*
− *Real* corresponding to the UML type *double*
− *String* corresponding to the UML type *string*
− *UnlimitedNatural* corresponding to the UML type *nonNegativeInteger.*

2.2 Pre and Post Conditions

A signature of a method is specified in a UML class by specifying the name of the method, its arguments along with their types, and the type of the result. However, there is no specification of the meaning of a method in a UML class. These specifications are given by OCL constraints called preconditions and postconditions.

Likewise, a message specifies the object to which it is sent (the receiver object), the method that should be invoked in response to the message and the actual arguments that contain specifics that pertain to the message. However, the meaning of the message is not specified.

In order to provide a declarative specification of a method, the context to which it applies must be specified first. This includes the name of the class of the receiver and the signature of the method to be invoked. For example, in the specification given below the method is *hire* of the class *Employee* and its argument is a company in which an employee should be hired. The precondition specifies that the collection of employees of the company given as the argument of this method does not already include the receiver of this message. This requires traversal of the relationship *employees* of the specified company and application of a method *includes* to test whether the receiver employee belongs to that collection of employees.

There are two postconditions of this method. The first ensures that the receiver of the message belongs to the collection of employees of the specified company. The second postcondition specifies that invocation of this method increases the number of employees of the specified company by 1. The second postcondition refers to the state of the company object before method execution using the keyword **pre**. So a postcondition in general relates two states: the state before and the state after method execution.

context Employee:: hire(c: Company)
 pre not (c.employees− >includes(self))
 post c.employees− >includes(self)
 post c.noOfEmployees=c.noOfEmployees@**pre** +1

The context for the method *fire* is also the class *Employee*. This method has no arguments and no result. The effect of this method is in changing the states of the receiver object and the associated company object obtained by traversing the *employer* relationship of the class *Employee*. The precondition requires that the receiver employee object belongs to the collection of employees of the associated company. This requires traversing two relationships, *employer* and then *employees*.

The first postcondition ensures that the receiver employee object is not any more in the collection of employees of the associated company object (the employer object). The second postcondition ensures that the number of employees of the associated employer company has been reduced by one. This postcondition requires a reference to the state prior to execution of the method *fire*. This is indicated by the keyword **pre**.

context Employee:: fire()
  pre self.employer.employees− >includes(self)
  post not(self.employer.employees− >includes(self))
  post self.employer.noOfEmployees=self.employer.noOfEmployees@**pre** - 1

Preconditions and postconditions are in UML diagrams specified as notes as illustrated in Fig. 2.3.

The context of the method *appointManager* is the class *Company* and the argument is an employee of that company to be appointed. The precondition requires that the specified object belongs to the collection of employees of the receiver company object. This requires traversal of the relationship   *employees*. The postcondition ensures that the CEO of the receiver company is the specified employee. This is accomplished by traversing the relationship CEO.

context Company:: appointManager(e: Employee)
  pre self.employees− >includes(e)
  post self.CEO = e

If a method has a result, it can be referred to in the postcondition using the key word *result* as in the example below:

context Company :: selectManager(): Manager
  post result = self.CEO

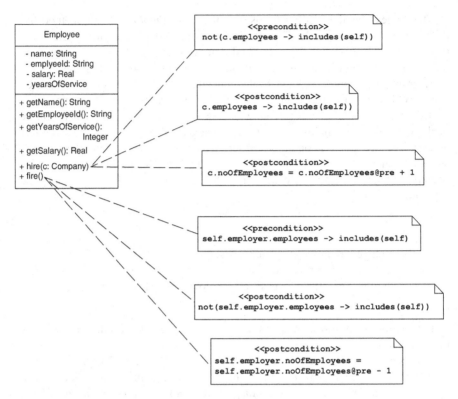

Fig. 2.3 Pre and post conditions in UML diagrams

2.3 Constraints over Collections

Collections are critical for the UML design methodology because associations require them. Constraints over collections require more complex expressions than those that are found in programming languages.

OCL has two types of quantifiers that apply to collections. The universal quantifier is denoted as **forAll**. It applies to all elements of a collection. In the invariant given below the collection to which the universal quantifier applies is the collection of all departments of a company which is obtained by traversing the relationship *departments*. d is a variable of type *Department* that ranges over that collection. The invariant holds if the manager of each department has salary greater than 100,000.

context Company **inv**:
  self.departments − > **forAll**(d: Department | d.manager.getSalary() > 100,000)

There are two simpler forms of the **forAll** expression. In the simplest one there is no iterator variable as in the example below:

context Company **inv**:
  self.departments − > **forAll**(manager.getSalary() > 100,000)

However, lack of an explicit iterator variable makes it impossible to define more complex **forAll** expressions. A more complex example of usage of the universal quantifier is the expression:

  forAll(e1,e2: Employee |
    e1.empoyeeId = e2.employeeId **implies** e1=e2)

which specifies that *employeeId* is a key in the collection of all employees. This condition holds if the equality of *employeeId* attributes of two employees implies that these are in fact equal employees. This expression is used in the invariant of the *Company* class as follows:

context Company **inv**:
  self.employees − > **forAll**(e1,e2: Employee |
    e1.empoyeeId = e2.employeeId **implies** e1=e2)

Invariants and pre- and postconditions for the class *Company* with the above constraint are shown in the UML diagram in Fig. 2.4.

The type of the iterator variable may be omitted because it can be inferred as the type of the elements of the underlying collection as in the following example:

context Company **inv**:
  self.departments − > **forAll**(d | d.manager.getSalary() > 100,000)

The existential quantifier is denoted by the keyword **exists**. An example of usage of this quantifier is an invariant of a class *Company* given below. It requires that there exists an employee of the company whose salary is greater than 100,000.

context Company **inv**:
  self.employees− >**exists**(e: Employee | e.getSalary() > 100,000)

Like in the case of the **forAll** expression, the simpler forms of the above invariant are:

context Company **inv**:
  self.employees− >**exists**(e | e.getSalary() > 100,000)

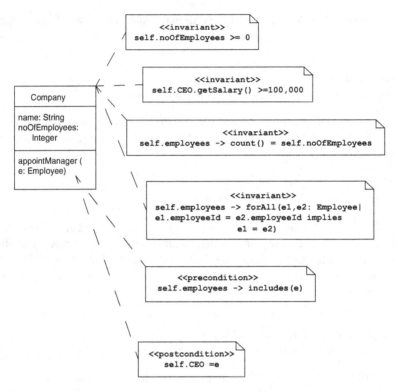

Fig. 2.4 Assertions for the class Company

context Company **inv**:
 self.employees− >**exists**(getSalary() > 100,000)

The universal and existential quantification may be composed as in the more complex invariants that follow. The invariant of the class *Company* specified below states that every department of the company has an employee whose salary is greater than 100,000.

context Company **inv**
self.departments − > **forAll**(d: Department |
    d.members − > **exists** (e: Employee | e.getSalary() > 100,000))

The invariant of the class *Company* given below specifies that the company has a department such that all of its employees have salary greater than 50,000.

context Company **inv**
self.departments − > **exists**(d: Department |
    d.members − > **forAll** (e: Employee | e.getSalary() > 50,000))

The value of an attribute may be specified by an OCL expression which determines the value of the attribute that will be computed (derived) from the values of other attributes. Here is an example:

context Company::noOfEmployees: Integer
  derive self.employees − > size()

OCL allows specification of operators in a declarative fashion. An example is an operator *maxSalary* associated with the class *Employee*. The result is specified by the postcondition which ensures that the result is greater than any employee salary.

context Company::maxSalary(): Real
  post self.employees − > **forAll**(e: Employee | result >= e.getSalary())

Methods that apply to class objects themselves rather than to individual objects of that class are called static. For example, the method *allInstances* is not a method that applies to individual objects but to the class itself. An example is the invariant of a class *Employee* which specifies that *emplyeeId* is a key for all instances of this class. This means that if two employees have equal employee ids they are in fact the same employee.

context Employee **inv**:
  Employee.allInstances()− >
  forAll(e1,e2: Employee |
     e1.employeeId=e2.employeeId **implies** e1=e2)

2.4   Selection of Collection Elements

Selection of elements of a collection that satisfy a given condition is in OCL specified using the *select* operator. For example, the expression given below:

  select(e:Employee | e.getSalary() > 50,000)

produces a collection of employees that have salary greater than 50,000. In this expression e is a variable of type *Employee* that ranges over a collection of employees and the expression *e.getSalary() > 50,000* specifies the condition that an employee object must satisfy in order to be selected. The invariant of the class *Company* given below shows how this operator is applied by traversing the relationship *employees* of the class *Company*.

context Company **inv**:
self.employees − > select(e: Employee | e.getSalary() > 50,000)− >notempty()

The operator *collect* allows projection of a collection to a new collection whose elements have selected components from the elements of the original collection. For example, the expression

collect(d:Department | d.noOfEmployees)

produces a collection whose elements are the numbers of employees in individual departments. In the invariant given below the expression

collect(d:Department | d.noOfEmployees)− >sum()

produces the sum of the numbers of employees of individual departments. The expression given below requires that this sum is equal to the number of employees of the company.

collect(d:Department | d.noOfEmployees)− >sum()=self.noOfEmployees

So we have the following invariant:

context Company **inv**:
self.departmets − >
collect(d:Department | d.noOfEmployees)− >sum()=self.noOfEmployees

Here is another example of an invariant that makes use of the *collect* operator:

context Company **inv**:
self.departments − > collect(d:Department |
    d.manager)− > subset(self.employees)

The above invariant specifies that the set of department managers is a subset of the set of employees.

2.5   Type Conformance

A flexibility called subtype polymorphism allows substitution of an instance of one type where an instance of its supertype is expected. This is possible only if the type conformance rules are satisfied. In the simple case of primitive types, the type *Integer* conforms to the type *Real* and the type *UnlimitedNatural* conforms to the type *Integer*. Hence an integer may be substituted where a real is expected and an unlimited natural may be substituted where an integer is expected. These are familiar rules.

Every type conforms to itself and in addition the type conformance is transitive, i.e., if type C conforms to type B and type B conforms to type A, then type C conforms to type A.

In the object-oriented paradigm subtype polymorphism is critical for the correct functioning of object-oriented software. A type defined by a subclass conforms to the type defined by its superclass. This way subtyping is tied to inheritance. The reason is that inheritance is monotonic, i.e., a subclass inherits all the properties (attributes and methods) of the superclass. This means that given the inheritance specified in Fig. 2.5, an instance of the class *Manager* may be substituted where an instance of the class *Employee* is expected.

Fig. 2.5 Type conformance
and inheritance

Because of this flexibility, the static, i.e. declared type of an object is in general different from its dynamic, i.e., run-time type. So if the static type of an object is *Employee*, its run-time type may in fact be *Manager* if a manager object is substituted for the employee object.

Collection types are critical for UML modeling philosophy because it relies heavily on the use of associations. The OCL hierarchy of collection types is given in Fig. 2.6. All the types in this figure are generic or parametric. The formal parameter T stands for the type of elements of a collection. A specific collection type is obtained by substituting the type of elements of that collection in place of the parameter *T*. For example, *Collection(Employee)* stands for the type which represents a collection of employees.

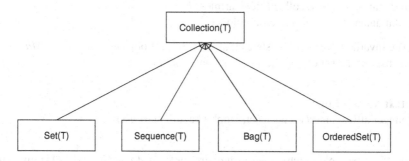

Fig. 2.6 Type conformance for collections

Collection is the most general collection type. Four collection types are derived by inheritance from the generic collection type *Collection(T)*. *Set(T)* fits the mathematical notion of a set. *Bag(T)* is a collection which, unlike *Set(T)*, may contain multiple elements of type *T*. *Ordered(Set)* is a type of a collection whose instances are ordered. *Sequence(T)* stands for a collection type which is linearly ordered hence represents a sequence.

The notion of type conformance allows viewing a collection of elements of type *B* as a collection of elements of type *A* as long as the type *B* conforms to the type *A* (Fig. 2.7). Specifically:

Fig. 2.7 Type conformance for collections

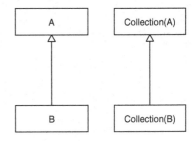

B conforms to *A* implies
Collection(B) conforms to *Collection(A)*
Set(B) conforms to *Set(A)*
Bag(B) conforms to *Bag(A)*
Sequence(B) conforms to *Sequence(A)*
OrderedSet(B) conforms to *orderedSet(A)*.

For example, in the invariant given below *Set(Manager)* is viewed as a set of type *Set(Employee)*, i.e.,

Set(Manager) conforms to *Set(Employee)*

context Company **inv**:
  self.departments − > collect(d:Department |
      d.manager)− > subset(self.employees)

The invariant given below states that the set of all objects of the class *Manager* is a subset of the set of all objects of the class *Employee*.

context Manager **inv**:
  Manager.allInstances()− >subset(Employee.allInstances())

Another example in which *Set(Manager)* conforms to *Set(Employee)* is given in the invariant given below:

context Department:: getDeptManagers(): Set(Employee) **inv**:
body
Department.allInstances()− >collect(d: Department | d.manager)

The idea of type conformance allows substitution of an object of type *Collection(B)* where an object of type *Collection(A)* is expected as long as *B* conforms to *A*. Although this rule for type conformance in OCL is intuitive, it is actually not type safe and it does not fit the notion of subtyping in typed object-oriented languages. As such, it creates nontrivial problems and hence it is not allowed in those languages. Even if *B* is a subtype of *A*, *Collection(B)* is not a subtype of *Collection(A)*. We will discuss these issues in detail in Chap. 3 and explain in more detail the relationship between parametric types and subtyping.

Viewing an instance of a class as an instance of its superclass is accomplished by type casts, as in the examples below:

context Manager **inv**:
self.employeeId=self.oclAsType(Employee).employeeId

The invariant of the class *Manager* specified below relates the salary attribute in the class *Employee* and in its subclass *Manager*.

context Manager **inv**:
self.getSalary() >= self.oclAsType(Employee).getSalary()

The above two cases are upcasts, i.e., their direction is up the inheritance hierarchy. OCL specifications are silent about down casts which are in fact typical for object-oriented languages. An example of a downcast is given in the following invariant.

context Employee **inv**:
self.getSalary() <= self.oclAsType(Manager).getSalary()

Down casts play an important role in object-oriented languages and they require dynamic checking to be discussed in Chap. 3.

2.6   Queries

Collection operators mimic the corresponding operators of the relational model of data. This is why OCL makes it possible to specify queries on collections. Those queries are defined as methods that operate on collection objects and in general return collections.

In the first example given below, a method *getDeptManagers* is defined in the context of a class *Company*. The result type of this method is *Set(Manager)*. The body of the method is defined in a declarative manner applying the operator *collect* to the collection of departments of the company which is the receiver of this method and collecting managers of individual departments.

context Company::getDeptManagers(): Set(Manager)
  body self.departments − > collect(d: Department | d.manager)

A query method *selectWellPaid* of a class *Company* returns a set of employees. Its body is defined using the operator *select*. This operator selects the well paid employees of the company object representing the receiver of this method.

context Company::selectWellPaid(pay: Real): Set(Employee)
  body self.employees − > select(e:Employee | e.getSalary() > pay)

In a query method *selectLargeCompanies* of the class *Company* the class method *allInstances* produces the collection of all companies and then those that have the number of employees larger than the argument size of this method.

context Company:: selectLargeCompanies(size: integer): Set(Company)
  body Company.allInstances − > select(c.Company | c.noOfEmployees > size)

A query method *wellPaid* of the class *Department* selects a set of employees of the department whose salary is greater than their manager's salary. This query involves traversal of the relationships *member* and *manager*.

context Department:: selectWellPaid(): Set(Employee)
  body self.members − >
    collect(e: Employee | e.getSalary() > self.employer.CEO.getSalary())

2.7 Operations on Collections

2.7.1 Collections

Type: Collection(T)

The notion of a collection in general allows multiple occurrences of the same element in a collection. The OCL type *Collection* has a function *count* which returns the number of occurrences of an element in a collection.

count(obj: T): Integer

The OCL type *Collection* also has a function *size* which computes the number of elements in a collection.

size(): Integer

A boolean function *includes* tests whether an element belongs to a collection. The meaning of this function is specified in its postcondition. In order for an element to belong to a collection its number of occurrences must be greater than 0.

context Collection(T)::includes(obj: T): Boolean
  post result = (self − > count(obj) > 0)

The boolean function *isEmpty* of the OCL type *Collection* tests whether the receiver collection is empty. This is specified in the postcondition of this function expressed in terms of the function *size*.

context Collection(T)::isEmpty(): Boolean
  post result = (self − > size()= 0)

2.7.2   Sets

Type: Set(T)
   The notion of a set does not allow multiple occurrences of the same element in a set. This is why the function *count* is redefined in the OCL type *Set* to ensure that the maximum number of occurrences of an element is 1.

context Set(T)::count(obj:T): Integer
  post result <= 1

The operations of inserting an element into a collection and deleting an element from a collection are defined as functions *including* and *excluding*. These functions construct a new set by inserting or deleting an element from the receiver set. The postcondition of the method *including* ensures that the resulting set contains all the elements of the initial (receiver) set and in addition it contains a newly inserted element.

context Set(T)::including(obj:T): Set(T)
  post result − >**forAll**(x:T | self− >includes(x) **or** x=obj)
  post self − >**forAll**(x:T | result− >includes(x))
  post result − > includes(obj)

The postcondition of the function *excluding* ensures that the resulting collection contains all the elements of the initial collection except the deleted element.

context Set(T)::excluding(obj:T)): Set(T)
  post result $-$ >**forAll**(x:T | self$-$ >includes(x) **and** (x <> obj))
  post self $-$ >**forAll**(x:T | result$-$ >includes(x)) = (x <> obj))
  post not (result $-$ > includes(obj))

The operation *union* of the type *Set* is defined in the usual manner by its postcondition. This postcondition guarantees that the elements of the resulting set belong to either the receiving or the argument set.

context Set(T)::union(s: Set(T)): Set(T)
  post result $-$ >**forAll**(x:T | self$-$ >includes(x) **or** s$-$ >includes(x))

The postcondition of the operation *intersection* ensures that the resulting set contains the elements that belong to both the receiver and the argument set.

context Set(T)::intersection(s: Set(T): Set(T)
  post result $-$ >**forAll**(x:T | self$-$ >includes(x) **and** s$-$ >includes(x))

Equality of two sets requires that each element in one set belongs to the other set and the other way around.

context Set(T):: =(s: Set(T): Boolean
  post result $-$ >**forAll**(x:T | self$-$ >includes(x) **and**
    s$-$ > **forAll** (x:T | s$-$ >includes(x))

Constraints associated with the type *Set(T)* are given in the UML diagram in Fig. 2.8.

2.7.3   Ordered Sets

Type: OrderedSet(T)
  The OCL type *OrderedSet* is equipped with a function *at* which returns the element at a specified position in the ordering. So the ordering is in fact linear. The precondition of this function requires that the integer specifying the position must be in the range of indices of the ordered set.

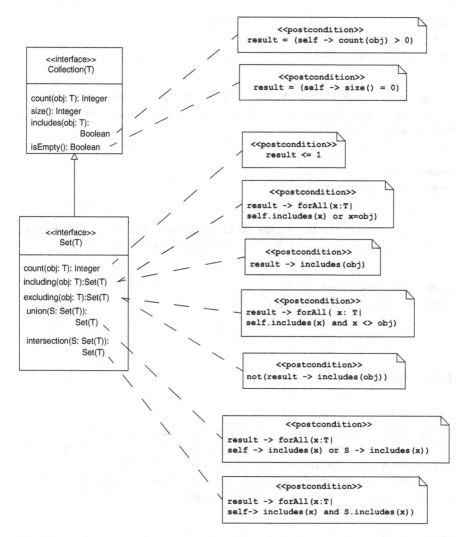

Fig. 2.8   Constraints for Set(T)

context OrderedSet(T)::at(i: Integer): T
pre i >= 1 **and** i <= self.size()

The function *indexOf* returns the position of the element specified as the argument of this function. The precondition of this function requires that the argument element belongs to the receiver set. The postcondition ensures that the argument element is indeed in the receiver set at the computed index. This condition is expressed in terms of the function *at*.

context OrderedSet(T):: indexOf(obj: T): Integer
 pre self.includes(obj)
 post self $-$ > at(result)= obj

Since the ordering is assumed to be linear, the function *first* returns the element of the receiver set at the first position. This is specified in the postcondition of this function using the function *at*.

context OrderedSet(T):: first(): T
 post result = self.at(1)

Likewise, the function *last* returns the last element of the receiver set. This is specified in the postcondition of this function using the functions *at* and *size*.

context OrderedSet(T):: last(): T
 post result = self.at(self $-$ > size())

2.7.4 Bags

Type: Bag(T)
 The notion of a bag differs from the notion of a set in that a bag may have multiple occurrences of the same element. The operation of inserting an element into a bag is defined as a function *including* which constructs a new bag from the receiver bag. In the resulting bag the number of occurrences of an element has been increased by one. The number of other elements remains the same as in the receiver bag.

context Bag(T):: including(obj:T): Bag(T)
 post result $-$ > **forAll**(x:T |
    if x=obj **then**
       result $-$ >count(x) = self $-$ > count(x) +1
    else result $-$ > count(x) = self $-$ >count(x)
 endIf)

The above example contains the OCL conditional expression. The operation *excluding* reduces the number of occurrences of the argument element in the resulting bag to zero. The number of occurrences of other elements remains the same.

context Bag(T):: excluding(obj:T): Bag(T)
  post result $->$ **forAll**(x:T |
    if x=obj **then**
      result $->$count(x) = 0
    else result $->$ count(x)= self$->$count(x)
  endIf)

An alternative to the above OCL definition would reduce by one the number of occurrences of the argument object if that object actually exists in the receiver bag.

The postcondition of the operation *union* of the OCL type *Bag* ensures that the number of occurrences of an element of the resulting bag is the sum of the numbers of occurrences of that element in the receiver and the argument bags of this operation.

context Bag(T):: union(bag: Bag(T)): Bag(T)
  post result$->$ **forAll** (x:T | result$->$count(x) =
    self $->$count(x) + bag$->$count(x))

The above OCL definition of the union of two bags is not the definition of this operation as defined in the algebra of bags. The alternative definition specifies that the number of occurrences of an element in the resulting bag is the maximum of the numbers of occurrences of that element in the two initial bags (the receiver and the argument bag in our case). The expression for the postcondition would then look like this:

  post result$->$ **forAll** (x:T | result$->$count(x) =
  self$->$count(x).max(bag$->$count(x)))

Unlike the OCL definition, this definition reduces to the notion of union of two sets if the given bags are in fact sets. In that case one would expect that the result of the operation of union is a set. So if these sets contain the same element x, it would appear only once in the result, whereas in the OCL definition it will appear twice.

The above reasoning is actually applied to the definition of the operation *intersection* of the OCL type *Bag*. The number of occurrence of an element of the resulting bag of this operation is the minimum of the numbers of occurrences of this element in the receiver and the argument bag.

context Bag(T):: intersection(bag: Bag(T)): Bag(T)
  post result$->$ **forAll** (x:T | result$->$count(x) =
    self$->$count(x).min(bag$->$count(x)))

The notion of equality of two bags specified by the operator $=$ requires that the two bags (the receiver and the argument bag) of this operation have the same

elements with the same number of occurrences, as specified in the postcondition of
this operation.

context Bag(T):: =(bag: Bag(T): Boolean
  post result = (self− > **forAll** (x:T |
    self− >count(x) = bag− >count(x)))

Constraints associated with the type *Bag(T)* are given in the UML diagram in
Fig. 2.9.

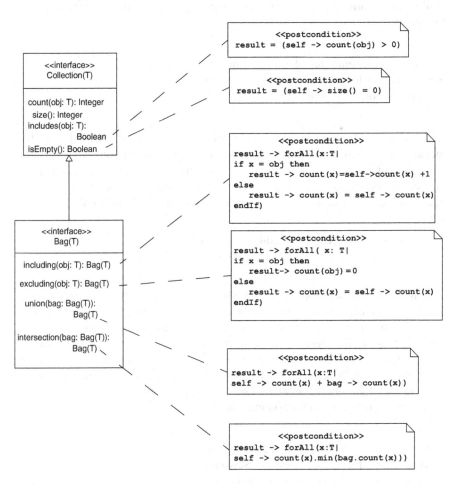

Fig. 2.9 Constraints for Bag(T)

Sequence(T)

The OCL type *Sequence* contains all the above defined functions of *OrderedSet*. The main difference between a sequence and an ordered set is that a sequence is not a set, i.e., it allows multiple occurrences of the same element.

2.8   Constraints and Inheritance

The OCL specifications are silent about the subtle interplay of inheritance and constraints. Consider an example of inheritance specified in Fig. 2.10.

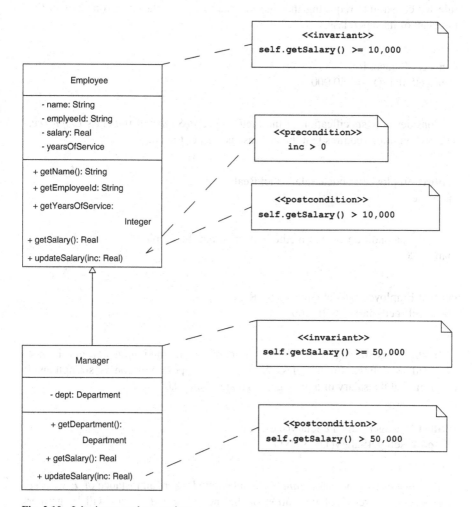

Fig. 2.10   Inheritance and constraints

The invariant of the class *Employee* requires that an employee salary is larger than or equal to 10,000.

context Employee **inv**
  self.getSalary() >= 10,000

The class *Manager* inherits this invariant. In addition, it strengthens it requiring that the salary of a manager is larger than or equal to 50,000. If an instance of *Manager* is substituted where an instance of *Employee* is expected, the substituted manager will behave as expected from an employee because the manager's invariant is stronger, i.e., if it holds, so will the invariant of an employee. This explains the rule for constraints requiring that the invariant of a subclass is stronger than the invariant of its superclass.

context Manager **inv**
  self.getSalary() >= 50,000

Consider now specification of the method *updateSalary* of the class *Employee*. The precondition requires that the increase is greater than 0.

context Employee:: updateSalary(inc: Real)
  pre inc > 0

The postcondition of this method ensures that the employee's salary is greater than 10,000.

context Employee:: updateSalary(inc: Real)
  post self.getSalary() > 10,000

In the class *Manager* the precondition of the method *updateSalary* is just inherited as defined for the class *Employee*. The postcondition is strengthened ensuring that the salary of a manager is greater than 50,000.

context Manager:: updateSalary(inc: Real)
    post self.getSalary() > 50,000

If an instance of the class *Manager* is substituted where an instance of *Employee* is expected, the result of invocation of the method *updateSalary* will be greater than 50,000 because it is the method *updateSalary* of the class *Manager* that will be invoked. The reason is that method selection in object-oriented languages is based on the run-time type of the receiver object which is *Manager*. But the effect of invocation of the method *updateSalary* of the class Manager satisfies the postcondition of the method *updateSalary* as defined in the class *Employee*. This explains the rule that method postconditions can be strengthened in a subclass.

Let us now try to strengthen the precondition of the method *updateSalary* in the class *Manager* requiring that a manager must have more than 2 years of service in order to get a salary update.

context Manager:: updateSalary(inc: Real)
   pre self.getYearsOfService()> 2
   post self.getSalary() > 50,000

Now a substitution of an instance of type *Manager* where an instance of type *Employee* is expected causes a behavioral incompatibility. A user of the class *Employee* is aware only of the precondition that requires that the increase must be positive. But it is the method *updateSalary* of the class *Manager* that will be executed and it will fail, because its precondition is not satisfied. This is why the rules for constrains require that the precondition of a method inherited from the superclass remains the same in the subclass.

The above rules are in fact followed in the specification of OCL operations on collections. Preconditions are never changed and postconditions are often strengthened.

2.9   Exercises

1. Specify in OCL the preconditions and the postconditions of the methods *buyAsset* and *sellAsset* of a UML class *Investor* specified in Chap. 1.
2. Specify in OCL a UML class *Asset* defined in Chap. 1 which asserts that *assetId* is a key in the collection of all instances of the class *Asset*.
3. Specify in OCL an invariant of the class *Broker* defined in Chap. 1 which asserts that all assets of the portfolios managed by an individual broker belong to the collection of all assets as seen by that broker.
4. Specify an invariant of a UML class *Portfolio* defined in Chap. 1 which asserts that each asset of a portfolio belongs to the collection of all assets seen by the broker of that portfolio.
5. Specify a class invariant of a UML class *Broker* defined in Chap. 1 which asserts that the assets of the portfolios managed by each individual broker belong to the collection of all assets seen by that broker.
6. Specify an invariant of a UML class *Investor* defined in Chap. 1 which asserts that the portfolio of an individual investor belongs to the collection of portfolios managed by the broker of that investor.

7. Specify an invariant of a UML class *Portfolio* defined in Chap. 1 which asserts that the total value of a portfolio is the sum of values of stocks and bonds in that portfolio.
8. Specify constraints of UML classes *Asset*, *Stock* and *Bond* defined in Chap. 1 in such a way that stocks and bonds behave like assets. That is, they satisfy all constraints of the class *Asset*.
9. Specify entity types in the Flight management application as UML classes.
10. For the invariants of the class *Flight* specified in the previous exercise specify the invariant of the class *Flight*.
11. Specify the preconditions and the postconditions of the methods *scheduleFlight* and *cancelFlight* of the class *FlightSchedule* specified above.
12. With the specification of classes produced in the previous exercises specify the preconditions and the postconditions of the methods *makeReservation* and *cancelReservation*.
13. Specify an invariant of the class *FlightSchedule* which asserts that each scheduled flight refers to the collection of all flights associated with the flight schedule.
14. Specify an invariant of the class *FlightSchedule* which asserts that the origin and the destination of each scheduled flight refer to the collection of all airports associated with the flight schedule.

Chapter 3
Implementation Technology

UML interfaces and classes are abstractions suitable for the design phase. These notions will eventually be mapped to the corresponding notions of the technology of object-oriented languages and systems that will be used to implement the designed model. In this chapter we consider the core notions of object-oriented programming languages that are critical for correct implementation of models produced by the UML methodology.

UML models specify relationships among entity types as associations or inheritance. Object-oriented programming languages have an explicit and very elaborate support for inheritance which is the core idea in these languages. However, object-oriented programming languages have no explicit support for associations.

We elaborate inheritance as it appears in object-oriented programming languages and its relationships to subtyping of entity types. Associations require parametric collection types and we elaborate how such types are supported in object-oriented programming languages. Subtyping of parametric collection types comes with subtleties not represented correctly in the OCL type conformance rules. We present techniques for representing associations using the described apparatus of object-oriented programming languages.

Typically, multiple use cases are executed concurrently. In Chap. 5 we will see how use cases are implemented as transactions. In this chapter we explain the basic apparatus of object-oriented programming languages that allows concurrent implementations of a model produced in the design phase.

© Springer International Publishing AG 2017   51
S. Alagić, *Software Engineering: Specification, Implementation, Verification*,
DOI 10.1007/978-3-319-61518-9_3

3.1   Objects and Classes

An abstract data type defines its instances entirely in terms of actions that can be performed upon those instances. An example is an abstract data type *IAsset* specified below as an interface. The actions are reading and setting the values of an instance of the *IAsset* type.

```
interface IAsset {
  float getValue();
  void setValue(float x);
}
```

The above definition is an abstraction offered to the users of the *IAsset* type. The users can only see the signatures of operations, i.e., their names, the types of their arguments, and the type of their result. All details of representation of instances of this type are hidden from the users. A representation of the *IAsset* type is given in the class *Asset* given below. The components of the object state are declared as private and the methods that either read or update the object state as public. This way the object state is encapsulated and accessible only by invoking public methods.

```
class Asset implements IAsset {
  private float value;
  public float getValue(){
    return value;
  }
  public void setValue(float value) {
    this.value=value;
  }
}
```

A UML diagram that corresponds to the above interface and its implementing class is given in Fig. 3.1.

Instances of a class are objects. An object has three defining components:

- object identity
- object state
- methods applicable to the object

When an object is created a unique identity is assigned to the object. Details of representation of the object identity are hidden from the users of the object.

In the example below expressions *a.setValue(5)* and *a.getValue()* are called messages.

```
Asset a; float value;
a.setValue(10,000);
value = a.getValue();
```

Fig. 3.1 UML interface and
its implementing class

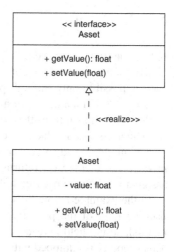

In general, invoking a method *m* of a class *C* whose signature is
B m(A1,A2,...,An), where *B, A1, A2, ...,An* are types, is called a message and
it has the form

a.m(a1,a2,...,an)

where the type of *a* is *C* and the type of *ai* is Ai for i=1,2 ...,n. The object *a*
in the above message is called the receiver of the message and *a1, a2, ...,an* are
arguments. All an object *x* needs to know in order to invoke a message on an object
a is the interface of the type of *a* as in the example above.

Object-oriented languages have a special keyword (like *self* in OCL or *this* in
Java and C#) to denote the receiver of a message. In the above example of *Asset* class
the method *setValue* refers to the value of the receiver object using the keyword *this*.
This is also necessary in order to distinguish the value of the formal parameter and
the value of the corresponding field of the receiver object. In the method *getValue*
the value of the field of the receiver object is referred to directly by its name so that
this is implicit.

Objects are created dynamically by invoking a class constructor as in the example
below:

Asset a=**new** Asset();
a.setValue(10,000);
float value = a.getValue();

In the above example a no argument constructor is invoked initializing the
Asset object to the default values for the types of components of the object state.
Additional constructors are typically defined for a class that would specify a
particular initialization of the object state as in the following example.

Asset(float value) {
 this.value = value;
}

Asset a= **new** Asset(10,000);

3.2 Properties

In the examples so far we followed a sound object-oriented design methodology to hide the components of the object state making its fields private. Access to the object state is possible only through public methods. This methodology has an explicit support in C# in the notion of a property. A property is a pair of public methods: a method *get* which returns the value of a component of the object state and a method *set* which assigns a value to a component of object state. In the simplest case this idea is implemented in such a way that a property has a backing field which is private. The method *get* returns the value of the backing field and the method *set* assign a value to the backing field.

In the example below the class *Asset* has two properties: *Name* and *Value*. The backing field of the property *Name* is *name* and this property has only the get method, so the field is read only. The backing field of the property *Value* is *value*. This property is equipped with a pair of methods: *get* and *set*. The argument of the method *set* is denoted by the keyword value, hence we had to use the expression this.value to refer to the backing field that has the same name. In C# default access right is private, but we explicitly denoted the backing fields as such.

```
class Asset {
  private String name;
  private float value;
  // other fields
  // constructor
  public String Name
  {    get { return name; } }
  public float Value
  {    get { return value; }
       set { this.value = value; }
  }
  // other poperties
}
```

Externally, a property is treated as a field. For example:

```
Asset a=new Asset;
a.Value = 100,000;
float assetValue=a.Value;
```

The notion of a property is not necessarily tied to a backing field. The result of the method *get* may be computed in a more complicated manner rather than by just reading the value of the backing field. Here is a modified class *Asset* which shows this for the property *Value*.

```
class Asset {
  private String name;
  private float purchaseValue;
  private float appreciation;
  // other fields
  // constructor
  public String Name
  {    get { return name; }
  public float Value
  {    get { return purchaseValue + appreciation; }
  }
  // other properties
}
```

3.3   Inheritance

A core feature of object-oriented languages allows specification of new types by derivation from the already defined types. This is how software reuse is accomplished in object-oriented technology. An example is a type *IStock* defined as an extension of the type *IAsset*:

```
interface IStock extends IAsset {
  public String getName();
  public void setName(String name);
  public String getCode();
  public void setCode(String code);
}
```

Instances of the type *IStock* inherit all methods of the base type *IAsset*. Additional methods of the type *IStock* that are specific to those objects are defined in the specification of the type *IStock*.

The class that implements the interface *IStock* specifies the additional components of the *Stock* object state along with the associated methods:

```
class Stock extends Asset
          implements IStock {
  private String name;
  private String code;
  public String getName(){
      return name;
  }
  public void setName(String name) {
```

```
    this.name=name;
public String getCode(){
    return code;
}
public void setCode(String code) {
    this.code=code;
}
}
```

The class *Stock* inherits the implementation of *Asset* objects and implements the methods whose signatures are specified in the interface *IStock*. In UML this situation is represented by the diagram in Fig. 3.2.

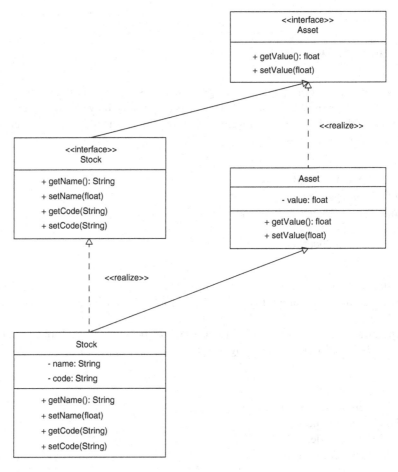

Fig. 3.2 UML diagram with diamond inheritance

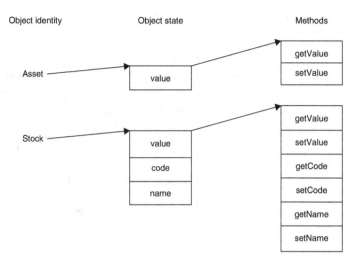

Fig. 3.3   Object states and methods

The states and the associated methods of objects of types *Asset* and *Stock* are represented in Fig. 3.3.

The basic features applicable to all object types are specified in the class *Object*. The details of representation of this class are not exposed to the users. A simplified specification of the class *Object* that omits signatures of other methods is given below.

```
public class Object {
 public boolean equals(Object x);
 public Class getClass();
 // other methods
}
```

All classes implicitly inherit from the class *Object*. The two methods whose signatures are specified above make it possible to test whether two objects are equal and to access the class information available at run time.

The inheritance relationships in our example are represented in Fig. 3.4. This diagram illustrates the type of multiple inheritance allowed in Java and C#.

A class can have a single superclass, and the root class *Object* has none. Multiple inheritance for classes is not allowed because it creates problems since a class specifies an implementation. If a class extends two different and independently developed classes, the question is which implementation is being inherited. A particularly problematic situation occurs in the case of diamond inheritance illustrated in Fig. 3.5. All the types in this diagram cannot be classes. A class can implement multiple interfaces. An interface can extend multiple interfaces because interfaces do not contain implementation. The only conflict that may occur is with names

Fig. 3.4 Inheritance for
interfaces and classes

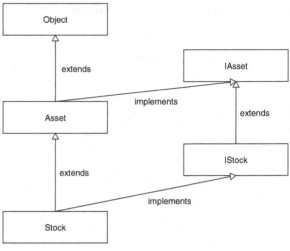

Fig. 3.5 Multiple
inheritance

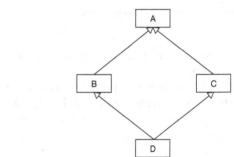

and signatures of methods inherited from multiple superinterfaces. These issues are
easily resolved with simple rules that Java and C# have. In the above example the
class *Stock* extends the class *Asset* and implements an interface *IStock*.

The immutable class object contains run-time representation of signatures of the
class fields, constructors and methods. The method *getSuperClass* applied to a class
object produces a reference to the superclass object. This makes the complete type
hierarchy of classes available at run-time. However, this hierarchy of types can be
only introspected, and not changed at run time. This is why the class *Class* contains
only introspection methods and cannot be extended (it is final). Changing at run
time the type information produced in the process of compilation would completely
defeat the purpose of a type system.

```
public final class Class {
  // methods for accessing field signatures
  // methods for accessing constructor signatures
  // methods for accessing method signatures
  public Class getSuperClass();
}
```

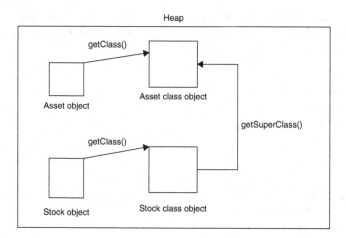

Fig. 3.6 Objects and class objects

The relationships between objects and their class objects is represented in Fig. 3.6. Objects and class objects are stored in the memory area called the heap. The heap allows dynamic creation of objects and memory management when objects are not in use any more.

3.4 Subtyping

The basic form of inheritance presented so far amounts to extension of both components of the object state, and the set of the associated methods. A subclass inherits all of them just the way they are defined in the superclass. This makes it possible to have a particular flexibility in object-oriented languages. An instance of a subclass could be safely substituted where an instance of the superclass is expected. This is not a literal substitution of the object representation. Substitution applies to object identities that are implemented as references to object states. A reference to an object of the superclass is replaced by a reference to an object of the subclass.

The general term polymorphism applies to situations like this where an instance of one type is substituted where an instance of a different type is expected. The form of polymorphism that is associated with inheritance is called subtype polymorphism. Although these two notions are in general different, they are identified in mainstream typed object-oriented languages. That is, the typing rules for deriving a subclass from another class by inheritance guarantee that the subclass defines a subtype of the superclass.

The most restrictive implementation of the rule for method subtyping is that an inherited method has exactly the same signature in a subclass as it does in the superclass. So the name, the types and the number of arguments and the result type

will be the same. A more flexible type safe discipline is that the argument types of
an inherited method remain the same as in the superclass and the result type may be
changed to the subclass type. For example:

```
public class Object {
  boolean equals(Object x)
  public Object clone()
// other methods
}
```

```
public class Asset {
  boolean equals(Object x)
  public Asset clone()
// other methods
}
```

3.5   Static and Dynamic Type Checking

The flexibility introduced by subtype polymorphism makes the declared (static) type
of an object in general different from its run-time (dynamic) type. The run-time type
is in general a subtype of the static type. For example:

```
Asset a = new Asset();
Stock s = new Stock();
a=s;
```

The static type of a is *Asset* and after the assignment $a = s$ its run-time type
is *Stock*. This has implications on selection of the most appropriate method when
executing a message. Consider the class *Stock* given below. In the notation used in
this book the symbol $=$ is overloaded. It stands for the standard mathematical notion
of equality as in the code below, as well as for the assignment as in Java and C#.

```
public class Stock {
  private String code;
  public boolean equals(Object x) {
      return (code = (Stock)x.code);
  }
// other methods
}
```

The method *equals* in the root class *Object* is defined as the test on object identity.
This is the only meaningful way of defining the equality of objects in general. That
is, two objects are equal if they have the same identity. In a specific class a more

suitable meaning of equality may be more appropriate. In the above class two stocks are considered equal if their codes are equal. So the method *equals* is redefined accordingly in the class *Stock*. This redefinition of an inherited method is called overriding.

Note that the signatures of the inherited method arguments are required to remain the same in the subclass. This creates an awkward situation because in the class *Stock* we would like to refer to the code field of the argument, and *Object* does not have such a field. This is why the type cast *(Stock)x* specifies that the intent is to view *x* as a *Stock*. There is no way to verify this cast statically, hence a dynamic check is generated by the compiler. This is an instance of dynamic type checking.

If a dynamic type check fails, it creates an exception. If the type cast *(Stock)x* fails, it will create a *ClassCastException*. The exception should then be handled properly as in the revised version of the class *Stock* given below.

```
public class Stock {
  private String code;
  public boolean equals(Object x) {
  try
      {return (code = (Stock)x.code); }
  catch (ClassCastException CastEx)
      { return false; }
  }
  // other methods
}
```

Exceptions may be structured in a type hierarchy. This is very useful because it allows separation of modeling regular behavior from modeling exceptional events. An example of a possible user defined inheritance hierarchy of exceptions is given in Fig. 3.7.

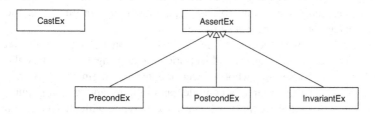

Fig. 3.7 Modeling exceptions

3.6 Dynamic Binding

In order for overriding to work correctly the method to be invoked is determined by the dynamic type of the receiver object. This is called dynamic dispatch of methods and it represents the most important case of dynamic binding in object-oriented languages. For example,

Object x = **new** Object();
Object y = **new** Object();
Stock s1 = **new** Stock();
Stock s2 = **new** Stock();
x=s1; y=s2;
... x.equals(y)...

The method to be invoked in response to the message x.equals(y) will be the method *equals* overridden in the class *Stock* because the run time type of *x* is *Stock*.

There are situations in which overriding a method should not be allowed. An example is the method *getClass* of the root class *Object*. This method has a particular implementation in the underlying virtual platform, which guarantees that invocation of this method will indeed return the class object of the receiver of the method. Allowing overriding would have serious implications on the intended semantics of this method creating nontrivial problems in dynamic type checking. This is why the method *getClass* is declared as final.

public class Object {
 public final Class getClass();
 // other methods
}

The class *Class* is final, which means that it cannot be extended, and hence none of its methods can be overridden. Since the class *Class* has only introspection methods, this guarantees safety of the type system at run-time, i.e., the type information cannot be mutated at run time.

Dynamic dispatch (selection) of methods based on the type of the receiver object is the basic technique in object-oriented languages. It brings the type of flexibility that makes the whole object-oriented paradigm work. Adding new types by inheritance to an already compiled and running application requires only compilation and linking of the newly introduced types without recompiling the existing application. However, this flexibility comes with some penalty in efficiency because the decision about method selection is postponed to runtime. Modern languages have efficient techniques for dynamic dispatch of methods, but some languages like C++ and C# try to avoid the associated cost by providing a static binding (method selection) option. In C#, methods are statically bound unless they are explicitly declared as *virtual*. For example, using our notation, the method *equals* which is intended to be overridden would be declared as follows:

```
public class Object {
  public virtual boolean equals(Object x);
  // other methods
}
```

Overriding this method in C# will be indicated by an explicit keyword **override**.

```
public class Stock {
  private String code;
  public override boolean equals(Object x) {
      return (code = (Stock)x.code);
  }
  // other methods
}
```

Methods whose receiver is the class object are always bound statically. The reason is that there is only one class object for all objects of that class. Since the receiver is known at compile time, there is no need to postpone method selection to run time. These methods are thus declared as static to indicate that they belong to the class itself. An example is the method *valueOfAllAssets* of the class *Asset*. The value of all assets is not the property of individual asset objects. It is the property of all objects of the class *Asset*, hence it belongs to the class itself.

```
public class Asset {
  // fields;
  public static float valueOfAllAssets();
  // other methods
}
```

True object-oriented design methodology makes components of an object state private and exposes public methods to be used to perform actions on the objects. A class this way looks like an abstract data type. The only way to perform operations on instances of an abstract data type is by invoking operations associated with that type. As explained earlier, this idea has explicit support in the C# notion of a property. An example of a property is given below:

```
public class Asset {
  private float totalValue;
  public float TotalValue
  { get {return totalValue;}
    set {totalValue = value; }
  }
}
```

A property may be used as if it is a field as illustrated below:

Asset a = **new** Asset();
a.TotalValue = 50,000;
a.TotalValue = a.TotalValue+20,000;

In the following example the value of a property is computed rather than being just the value of a backing field.

```
public class Asset {
  private float unitValue;
  private int numberOfShares;
  public float TotalValue
  { get {return unitValue * numberOfShares; }
  }
}
```

We summarize the above discussion as follows:

– The basic mechanism for selecting a method for executing a message (method dispatch) in object-oriented languages is dynamic. It is based on the run-time type of the receiver object.
– The receiver of a static (i.e. class) method is the class object. Since there is only one class object of a given type, selection of a static method is static.
– Some languages (C++ and C#) allow a choice of static versus dynamic method dispatch. Although this is done for the reasons of efficiency, it has been shown that when both dispatch mechanisms are used in a program, that may obscure the meaning of the program.

3.7 Abstract Classes

Structuring an implementation of an object-oriented model as a hierarchy of abstractions has significant advantages. The top level of this hierarchy consists of interfaces that are exposed to the users of the system as they define messages that the users can send. The implementation details are completely hidden from the users of the system.

```
interface IAsset {
  String getName();
  float getTotalValue();
}
```

The next level of abstraction consists of classes implementing the specified interfaces. However, this implementation level can also often be structured as a hierarchy. The first level of this hierarchy are abstract classes. An abstract class is a partially implemented class, that is, some aspects of implementation are left to the lower level classes derived by inheritance. An abstract class has at least one abstract method, i.e., a method whose signature (name, arguments and result) is specified at the level of the abstract class. However, the implementation details can be specified only in a class derived by inheritance from the abstract class. The reason is that the derived class contains the specifics required to implement an abstract method.

An example of an abstract class that implements the interface *IAsset* given above is *FinancialAsset*. It specifies the implementation details related to the name of an asset, but the method *getTotalValue* can be implemented only when we actually know the specifics of a particular financial asset type. This is why this method is declared as abstract.

```
abstract class FinancialAsset implements IAsset {
  private String name;
public String getName()
  { return name ; }
public abstract float getTotalValue();
}
```

Likewise, an abstract class *RealEstateAsset* that implements the interface *IAsset* contains some implementation details and it has an abstract method *getTotalValue* whose implementation can be specified only when the specifics of a particular type of a real estate asset is known.

```
abstract class RealEstateAsset implements IAsset {
  private String name;
  private City location;
public String getName()
  { return name; }
public City getLocation()
  { return location ; }
public abstract float getTotalValue();
}
```

Since an abstract class is partially implemented, it is not possible to create an object of an abstract class. It is only possible to create objects of a fully implemented class. If such a class is derived by inheritance from the abstract class, the created object will be also of the abstract class type by subtype polymorphism.

An abstract class is not the same as an interface. An interface contains only the signatures of methods. An abstract class contains partial implementation (fields, implemented methods). An abstract class is different from an interface even if it consists of abstract methods only. It is still a class and single inheritance applies to it whereas multiple inheritance applies to interfaces. Finally, all methods of an interface are public. An abstract class may have public, private and protected fields and methods.

The bottom level of the implementation hierarchy consists of classes with all details specified and implemented. In the class *Stock* given below an implementation of the method *getTotalValue* is specified using specific features of this class.

```
class Stock extends FinancialAsset {
  private float shareValue;
  private int noOfShares;
public float getTotalValue()
  { return shareValue * noOfShares; }
}
```

Likewise, the method *getTotalValue* is implemented in the class *House* based on the specific attributes of a house which in general do not belong to all financial assets.

```
class House extends RealEstateAsset {
  private float marketValue;
  private float mortgage;
public float getTotalValue()
  { return marketValue – mortgage; }
}
```

There are several advantages of structuring an implementation as the above described hierarchy. One of them is that the implementation is easier to understand and manage when evolution is required over time. Pushing the implementation details to the lower levels allows changes of the implementation details without affecting the upper levels, the user interfaces in particular.

3.8 Collection Types

Most object-oriented languages are equipped with the root class *Object* (C++ is a notable exception). The class *Object* along with subtype polymorphism allows specification of *Collection* type whose elements are simply objects. In fact, this was the only way of specifying a generic collection type in the initial versions of Java and C#:

```
public interface Collection{
  public boolean isMember(Object x);
  public void add(Object x);
  public void remove(Object x);
}
```

An object of type *Collection* is equipped with methods for testing whether an object belongs to the collection, inserting new objects into the collection, and deleting objects from the collection. The main problem with this specification is that objects of any type may be inserted into a collection defined this way. If we would like to define a specific collection, like a collection of assets, we would do it as follows:

Collection assets;

So the following type checks:

Stock s = **new** Stock();
assets.add(s);

However, so does the following

Collection stocks;
Bond b = **new** Bond();
stocks.add(b);

The reason is that both *Stock* and *Bond* are subtypes of *Object*, and so is any other object type. The other problem occurs when getting objects from a collection as in the *for* statement below. This statement introduces a control variable *s* of type *Stock* and iterates over the collection *stocks*. In the process the control variable assumes the values of the elements of the collection *stocks*.

for (Stock s: stocks)
  s.setValue(50,000);

The above code will not compile in Java because the control variable *s* is declared to have the type *Stock*, and the elements of the collection *stocks* are of type *Object*. Let us modify the above loop to correct this type mismatch as follows:

for (Object s: stocks)
  s.setValue(50,000);

The above will not type check either because the class *Object* is not equipped with a method *setValue*. This is why a type cast is necessary:

for (Object s: stocks)
  (Stock)s.setValue(50,000);

This type cast looks redundant, but it is necessary because an object retrieved from a collection of stocks may not be a stock at all. So not only is a dynamic check necessary, but it may fail at run-time as well. There is really no good solution for this situation. In order to avoid program failure the original code must be extended with exception handling as follows. This is hardly an attractive way to specify an iteration over a collection of stock objects.

```
try {
    for (Object s: stocks)
    (Stock)s.setValue();
    }
catch (ClassCastException classEx )
    {exception handling }
```

The notion of a set of objects may be defined using subtype polymorphism as follows:

```
public interface Set extends Collection {
  public Set union(Set s);
  public Set intersection(Set s);
}
```

The difference between a collection in general and a set is that an element may belong multiple times to a collection. The notion of a set does not allow this: an element is either a member of a set or it is not. This is why an element cannot be inserted into a set if it already belongs to the set. The behavior of delete is also different for collections and sets. Deleting an object from a set means that the object does not belong to the set. Because of possible multiple occurrences of an object in a collection, that would happen only if the last occurrence is deleted. In addition, sets are equipped with operations such as *union* and *intersection* that collections in general do not have (Fig. 3.8).

A bag is a collection that keeps explicit count of the number of occurrences of each element that belongs to the bag. In addition, a bag is equipped with operations such as *union* and *intersection*. The semantics of these operations are defined in such a way that they reduce to the semantics of *union* and *intersection* for sets in a particular case of a bag that is in fact a set.

The rule for union of bags is the following. If an element x belongs m times to a bag $B1$ and n times to a bag $B2$, then x will belong $max(m,n)$ times to the union of

Fig. 3.8 Collection types

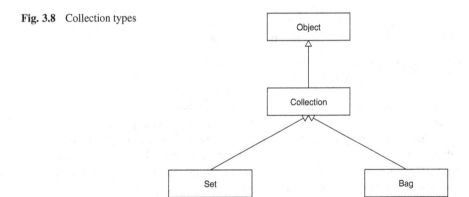

B1 and *B2*. This definition comes from the algebra of bags and it is different from the definition of this operation in OCL. Symmetrically, *x* will belong *min(m,n)* times to the intersection of *B1* and *B2*. This definition agrees with the OCL definition.

3.9   Parametric Types

The problems in specifying collection types using subtype polymorphism are avoided by a different form of polymorphism called parametric polymorphism. Using this form of polymorphism the notion of a collection is specified as follows.

```
public interface Collection<T> {
public boolean isMember(T x);
public void add(T x);
public void remove(T x);
}
```

The interface *Collection* now has a type parameter T. T stands for any object type, so that there is an implicit quantification over all object types. Collection <T> may be viewed as a template for construction of new types by substitution. Substituting *Stock* for the type parameter T produces a collection of stocks type denoted as:

Collection<Stock>

The previous code obtains the following form:

```
Collection<Stock> stocks;
Stock s = new Stock();
stocks.add(s)
```

However, the following will not type check, i.e., it will produce a compile-time error.

```
Collection<Stock> stocks;
Bond b = new Bond();
stocks.add(b)
```

Accessing elements of the collection of employees does not require a type cast. So a previous *for* statement will now type check:

```
for (Stock s: stocks)
s.setValue(50,000);
```

The key property of parametric polymorphism is that it allows static (i.e., compile-time) type checking. The unfortunate consequences of dynamic type checks are completely avoided.

The universal form of parametric polymorphism does not allow static typing of a variety of other abstractions such as ordered collections, ordered sets etc. The problem with the definition of the type of ordered collections as:

OrderedCollection<T>

is that it does not guarantee that the object types substituted for T will be equipped with ordering. This is why the parametric type *OrderedCollection* is defined with a type constraint for the type parameter:

OrderedCollection<T **extends** Comparable<T>>

where the interface *Comparable* is equipped with a comparison method and defined as follows:

public interface Comparable<T> {
  public int compareTo(T x);
// other comparison methods
}

Parametric interface *OrderedCollection* is now specified as follows:

public interface OrderedCollection<T **extends** Comparable<T>>
         extends Collection<T> {
// ...
}

The above specification means that only types that extend or implement the interface *Comparable* will be acceptable as the actual type parameters of OrderedCollection<T **extends** Comparable<T>>. So if we have

Stock **implements** Comparable<Stock>

OrderedCollection<Stock> will satisfy the static type check.

The form of parametric polymorphism in which there is a bound on the type parameter is called bounded. When the bound itself is parametric, like in the above cases, the form of parametric polymorphism is called F-bounded.

Array is a parametric type with special notation and special properties. T[] is an array type for any specific type T. The form of parametric polymorphism is thus universal.

The interplay of parametric types and inheritance is nontrivial. We will show that type safe rule in fact contradicts the type conformance rules of OCL specified in Chap. 2. Assume that we have

class Stock **extends** Asset { ... } .

We know that this implies

Stock *subtypeOf* Asset

following the rules for the signatures of inherited fields and methods. The question is now whether this implies

Collection<Stock> *subtypeOf* Collection<Asset> ? ? ?

Fig. 3.9 Parametric types
and subtyping

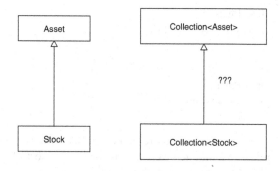

The answer is no. It is easy to see why. The signature of the method *add* in the class Collection<Asset> is *void add(Asset x)* and the signature of this method in the class Collection< *Stock* > is *void add (Stock x)*. This violates the typing rules for inherited methods. The argument signatures of an inherited method must remain the same as in the superclass.

Following the same argument we would have for array types:

Stock[] *notSubtypeOf* Asset[]

However, languages like Java and C# still allow substitution of objects of type Stock[] in place of an object of type Asset[]. This flexibility has pragmatic reasons. For example, an algorithm that sorts an array of persons would not be otherwise applicable to an array of employees. However, this relaxation of the static typing rules requires dynamic checks in order to prevent violation of subtyping at run-time, which both Java and C# have.

3.10 Representing Associations

UML analysis and design methodology relies heavily on associations. However, object-oriented languages do not have an explicit support for associations quite unlike inheritance. Associations are in object-oriented languages represented using the apparatus for complex objects and collection types. A complex object is an object that refers to other objects as its components.

The one to one association between objects of type *Investor* and *Portfolio* in Fig. 3.10 is represented in the their classes omitting the access specifications as follows:

Fig. 3.10 Associations

class Investor {
 Portfolio myPortfolio;
}

class Portfolio {
 Investor owner;
}

So an investor has a reference to the portfolio object of the investor and a portfolio refers to a unique investor as its owner . A portfolio object also refers to the broker object that manages that portfolio. The relationship between a broker object and portfolio objects is one to many, that is, a broker manages some finite unspecified number of portfolios. This relationship is specified using an instantiated parametric type *Collection<Portfolio>* (Fig. 3.11).

Fig. 3.11   Associations

class Portfolio {
 Investor owner;
 Broker manager;
}

class Broker {
 Collection<Portfolio> portfolios;
}

A portfolio consists of a collection of assets. Symmetrically, an asset object can participate in a number of portfolio objects. The relationship between portfolio objects and asset objects is thus many to many as in Fig. 3.12.

Fig. 3.12   Associations

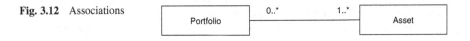

Representation of this relationship requires two *Collection* types: *Collection<Asset>* and *Collection<Portfolio>*.

class Portfolio {
 Collection<Asset> myAssets;
}

```
class Asset {
 Collection<Portfolio> portfolios;
}
```

Finally, since Stock and *Bond* are subtypes of *Asset*, in *Collection<Asset>* elements of this collection could be *Stock* or *Bond* objects, i.e., a portfolio consists of a collection of stocks and bonds. This is illustrated in Fig. 3.13.

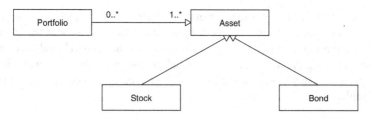

Fig. 3.13 Associations

```
class Stock extends Asset {
  ...
}
```

```
class Bond extends Asset {
  ...
}
```

It is important to understand that object-oriented languages have no explicit mechanism for managing associations. Their management is entirely up to the implementor who must provide the appropriate code.

3.11 Concurrent Implementations

3.11.1 Threads

Java introduced the notion that a thread of execution is an object. As such, it is created dynamically as all objects are. A thread object has a state (of execution) and it is equipped with methods that introspect and change the thread object state. This way a Java program can have multiple threads of execution that exist concurrently and contribute to the overall outcome of the program execution.

The core of the Java model of concurrent threads is based on the interface *Runnable* and the class *Thread*. The interface *Runnable* contains only one method *run*. Its implementation in a specific class specifies the actual thread execution process.

```
public interface Runnable {
  void run();
}
```

The class *Thread* has a constructor that takes a *Runnable* object as the argument and creates a thread of execution. The method *run* in the class *Thread* has an empty implementation so that it must be overridden in a specific class. Thread execution is started by invoking the method *start*. A thread execution can be interrupted, but the basic idea of the Java model is that all threads created by a program should run to their completion.

```
public class Thread
      extends Object, implements Runnable {
  public Thread(Runnable target);
  public void start();
  public void run();
  public void interrupt();
  // other methods
}
```

An example of using the interface *Runnable* and the class *Thread* is the class *TestRun* given below.

```
class TestRun implements Runnable {
  private float minWage;
  public TestRun(float minWage) {
      this.minWage = minWage;
  }
  public void run() {
  // get next employee wage larger than minWage
  ...
  }
}
```

In the code given below, an object of the class *TestRun* is created, as well as a new *Thread* object. The *Thread* constructor takes an object of *TestRun* as its argument. The newly created thread is then started.

```
TestRun p = new TestRun(15.00);
new Thread(p).start();
```

3.11.2 Synchronization

Existence of multiple concurrent threads that access objects creates some well-known problems. Actions of two threads performed concurrently on the same object may produce incorrect results such as incorrect updates or incorrect results of introspection of the object state. This is why concurrent access to objects must be controlled to avoid these problems.

A well known approach is illustrated below by the class *SynchronizedObject*. The methods that access and modify the hidden object state are declared as synchronized. This means that a thread executing one of these methods gets exclusive access to the underlying object state. The object state is made available to other threads when the method completes it execution. This basic model is extended with a more sophisticated synchronization protocol for concurrent threads accessing the same object.

```
public class SynchronizedObject {
  private Object state;
  public SynchronizedObject(Object initialState) {
      state=initialState;
  }
  public synchronized Object get() {
      return state; }
  public synchronized void set(Object obj) {
      state=obj ;}
  // methods inherited from Object:
  // public wait()
  // public void notifyAll()
  // other methods
}
```

The undesirable effect of unsynchronized access of two threads to the same object is illustrated in Fig. 3.14. The update of Thread 1 will be lost.

Fig. 3.14 Unsynchronized object access

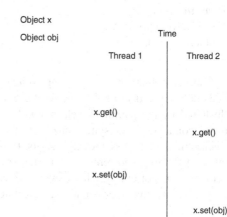

Fig. 3.15 Synchronized
object access

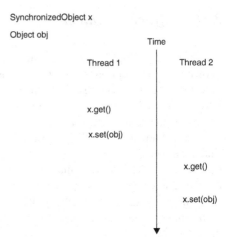

The effects of synchronized access that avoids the above problem is illustrated in Fig. 3.15.

An example of synchronization as it applies to portfolio objects is given below. Synchronization avoids problems of concurrent access of an investor and a broker to the same portfolio.

```
public class Portfolio {
  private Collection<Asset> assets;
  public Portfolio(Collection<Asset> assets) {
      this.assets = assets;
  }
  public synchronized void buyAsset(Asset a) {
      assets.include(a); }
  public synchronized void sellAsset(Asset a) {
      assets.exclude(a);}
  // methods inherited from Object:
  // public wait()
  // public void notifyAll()
  // other methods
}
```

A more sophisticated scheduling strategy for concurrent access is based on the methods *wait* and *notifyAll* inherited from the root class *Object*. This model is illustrated by the parametric class *SynchronizedContainer*. Adding new elements to the container by a synchronized method *add* works in accordance with the synchronization access model described above. The container is assumed to be unbounded. However, removing an element from the container is possible only if a container is not empty. This is why a thread that attempts to remove an element from an empty container is put in a wait state. The method *add* will send a message *notifyAll* to all waiting threads when it successfully adds an element to the container. One of those threads waiting for this message will be selected nondeterministically and its remove action will be performed.

```
class SynchronizedContainer<T> {
  private Container<T> container = new Container<T>;
  public synchronized void add(T x) {
      container.add(x);
      notifyAll();
}
  public synchronized void remove(T x) {
      throws InterruptedException;
{ while (container.size() = 0)
      wait();
      container.remove(x);
  }
}
```

3.11.3   Synchronization and Inheritance

Many classes are developed with no considerations for possible concurrent access to their objects. Producing a class that allows concurrent access from a class that does not is accomplished by inheritance. A class that enforces synchronized access is derived from the base class by overriding the inherited methods and declaring them as synchronized. The bodies of these synchronized methods can now just invoke the corresponding methods in the base class. This is illustrated by the classes *OrderedCollection* and *OrderedCollectionSync*.

The methods of the class *OrderedCollection* are those specified in the interface *Collection* which the class *OrderedCollection* implements. The representation of a sorted collection in the class *OrderedCollection* is a linked list, where *LinkedList* is an already defined parametric class. Methods of the class *OrderedCollection* are implemented by invoking methods of the class *LinkedList*. The main difference is in the method *add* which is overridden in such a way that insertion into the underlying linked list maintains the ordering of the sorted collection of elements. The type constraint T **extends** Comparable<T> guarantees that elements of the sorted collection are equipped with the method *compareTo*.

```
public class OrderedCollection<T extends Comparable<T>>
          implements Collection<T> {
private LinkedList<T> elements;
public OrderedCollection() {
      elements = new LinkedList<T>();
}
```

```
 public boolean isMember(Object e) {
     return elements.contains(e);
}
 public void add(T e) {
 if (! elements.contains(e)) {
 for (int i = 0; i < elements.size() - 1; i++) {
     if (elements.get(i).compareTo(e) ≤ 0 ∧
     elements.get(i + 1).compareTo(e) > 0)
     elements.add(e);
}
 public void remove(Object e) {
     if (elements.contains(e))
     elements.remove(e);
}
}
```

Note the general rule that the synchronized property of a method is not inherited. In this example, the methods in *OrderedCollection* are not synchronized, and their overridden versions in *OrderedCollectionSync* are synchronized. The class *OrderedCollectionSync* is derived by inheritance from the class *OrderedCollection* by overriding all the inherited methods, declaring them as synchronized, and invoking the methods in the superclass indicated by the usage of the key word *super*.

```
public class OrderedCollectionSync< T extends Comparable<T>>
           extends OrderedCollection<T> {
 public OrderedCollectionSync() { super(); }
@Override
 public synchronized boolean contains(Object e) {
 if (e <> null) {return super.contains(e); }
 else return false;
}
@Override
 public synchronized void add(T e) {
 super.add(e); }
@Override
public synchronized void remove(Object e) {
 super.remove(e); }
}
}
```

3.12 Exercises

1. Specify an implementation of the class *Stock* in a typed object-oriented language (such as Java or C#) in such a way that it implements the interface *IStock* and extends the class *Asset*.
2. Specify an interface *InvestorI* and it implementing class *Investor* making use of a typed object-oriented language.
3. Specify the interface *IPortfolio* and its implementing class *Portfolio* making use of appropriate parametric collection types for representing collections of stocks and bonds.
4. Specify an interface *IBroker* and its implementing class *Broker* with the same guidelines as in the above exercises.
5. Implement the notion of an investment bank as a complex object whose components are collections of assets, portfolios and brokers.
6. Specify and implement the method *equals* of the class *Asset*. Override this method in the classes *Stock* and *Bond* that implement these two subtypes of the type *Asset*.
7. Specify implementation of the class *Portfolio* using two techniques for representing collection types. In the first representation elements of a collection type are objects and in the second a collection type is parametric. Demonstrate the problems with the first representation and the advantages of the second.
8. Consider collection types Collection<Airport>, Collection<DomesticAirport> and Collection<InternationaAirport>. Assume that *DomesticAirport* and *InternationalAirport* are subtypes of *Airport*. Are Collection<DomesticAiport> and Collection<InternationalAirport> subtypes of Collection<Airport>?
9. Assuming that collections of assets, investors and brokers are ordered by their keys, implement the classes *Asset, Investor* and *Broker* using ordered collection types.
10. Specify and interface *IFlightShedule* using parametric ordered types for representing collections of flights, airports and aircraft.
11. Specify an interface *IRegistrar* using parametric ordered collection types for representing collection for courses, students, instructors and and classrooms.

Chapter 4
Mapping Models to Code

In this chapter we assume that we have the results of analysis and design consisting of the informal specification of the use cases along with the entity types involved in those use cases. We also assume that the inheritance and the association relationships among those entity types are also specified. In addition, we assume that the preconditions and the postconditions of the use cases are specified in an informal manner as in Chap. 1.

The first step in our methodology is specification of the results of the design as a collection of interfaces representing entity types and their relationships. This representation specifies what kind of messages objects in this application can send and receive. In addition, use cases and methods will be specified in OCL in terms of their pre and post conditions. This methodology produces a high level specification of the required software. The level of abstraction at this level is such that many details of the actual code are still left unspecified and will be elaborated in the subsequent step.

The second step in producing code implementing the designed model is specification of classes that implement the interfaces specified in the first step. At this level the procedural code in the chosen object-oriented programming language is produced in such a way that the constraints specified in the first step are satisfied. In Chap. 6 we will discuss the technology that makes it possible to verify that the code actually satisfies the constraints.

4.1 Specifying Interfaces

4.1.1 Investment Management Application

In specifying interfaces for the investment management model in Fig. 4.1 we specify the signatures of methods that allow traversal of the associations in that model.

© Springer International Publishing AG 2017
S. Alagić, *Software Engineering: Specification, Implementation, Verification*,
DOI 10.1007/978-3-319-61518-9_4

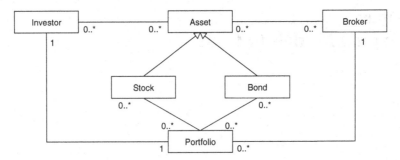

Fig. 4.1   Investment management entity types and their relationships

The interface *IAsset* has a method *getBrokers* that represents one side of the many to many association between the entity types *Asset* and *Broker*. The other side of this association is specified by the method *getAllAssets* of the interface *IBroker*. In addition, the interface *IBroker* has a method *getMyPortfolios* which represents one side of the one to many association between a broker and the portfolios that the broker manages. The interface *IPortfolio* has a method *getBroker* that represents the other side of this relationship and produces the broker of a portfolio.

```
interface IAsset {
float getPrice();
boolean priceOk();
Collection < Broker > getBrokers();
Collection< Portfolio > getPortfolios();
}
```

```
interface IBroker {
Collection<Asset> getAllAssets();
Collection <Portfolio> getMyPortfolios();
}
```

The method *getPortfolioAssets* represents one side of the one to many association between a portfolio and the assets that it contains. The method   *getInvestor* represents one side of the one to one relationship of a portfolio and its owner. The method *getBroker* represents one side of the one to many relationship between brokers and the portfolios that they manage.

```
interface IPortfolio {
Collection<Asset> getPortfolioAssets();
Broker getBroker();
Investor getInvestor();
}
```

The method *getMyPortfolio* of the interface *InvestorI* represents one side of the one to one relationship between an investor and its portfolio. The methods *buyAsset* and *sellAsset* of the interface *InvestorI* represent the corresponding use cases.

interface InvestorI {
Portfolio getMyPortfolio();
Broker getMyBroker();
Collection<Asset> getAllAssets();
void buyAsset(Asset a);
void sellAsset(Asset a);
}

The next step in our methodology is specification of constraints associated with the designed interfaces. We will do that just for the methods *buyAsset* and *sellAsset* of the interface *InvestorI* that represent the corresponding use cases. These constraints will be specified in OCL. This way we will produce a declarative specification of the implementation of the investment management model. This representation will be subject to further decomposition in which all implementation details of the procedural code will be developed.

The first precondition of the method *buyAsset* requires that the asset is not already in the investor's portfolio. This is a simplification of the real situation. The second precondition requires that the price of the asset is OK. The postcondition ensures that the asset is in the investor's portfolio. These pre and post conditions are specified in an UML diagram in Fig. 4.2.

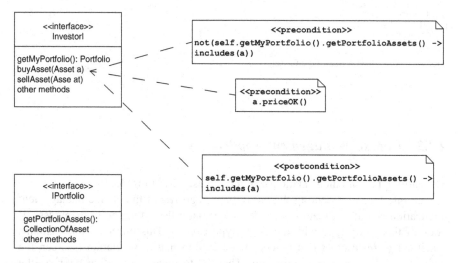

Fig. 4.2 Assertions for buying an asset

context InvestorI:: buyAsset(Asset a):
pre not (self.getMyPortfolio().getPortfolioAssets() − > includes(a))
pre a.priceOk();
post self.getMyPortfolio().getPortfolioAssets() − > includes(a)

The precondition of the method *sellAsset* is that the asset is in the investor's portfolio, and the postcondition that it is not any more.

context InvestorI:: sellAsset(Asset a):
pre self.getMyPortfolio().getPortfolioAssets() − > includes(a)
post not (self.getMyPortfolio().getPortfolioAssets() − > includes(a))

These pre and post conditions are specified in an UML diagram in Fig. 4.3.

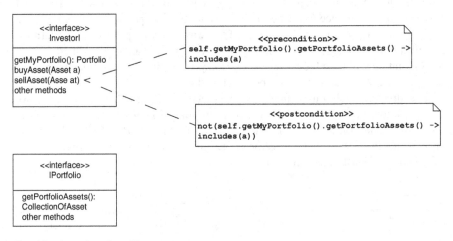

Fig. 4.3 Assertions for selling an asset

4.1.2 Course Management Application

The entity types and their relationships are represented in Fig. 4.4.

The interface representing the entity type *Registrar* of the course management application contains a method *getAllCourses* that reflects the one to many association of this entity type with the entity type *Course*. This interface also contains a method *getInstructors* that represents the one to many association between the entity types *Registrar* and *Instructor*. The one to many association between the entity types *Registrar* and *Student* is represented by the method *getStudents*. The method *getRooms* produces a collection of rooms available for scheduling.

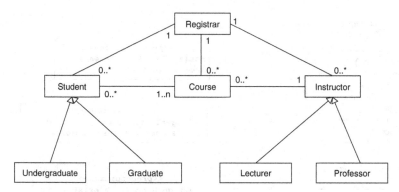

Fig. 4.4 Course management entities and their relationships

interface IRegistrar {
Collection<Course> getAllCourses();
Collection<Instructor> getInstructors();
Collection<Students> getStudents();
Collection<Room> getRooms();
void scheduleCourse(Course c);
void deleteCourse(Course c);
}

The methods *scheduleCourse* and *deleteCourse* specify the corresponding use cases. The first precondition of the method *scheduleCourse* requires that the course to be scheduled is not already scheduled. The second precondition requires that there is a suitable room for the course to be scheduled. The third precondition requires that there is an instructor suitable to be scheduled for the course. The postcondition ensures that the course is actually scheduled, i.e., it belongs to the collection of all scheduled courses.

context IRegistrar:: scheduleCourse(Course c):
pre not (self.getAllCourses() − > includes(c))
pre self.getRooms() − > **exists**(r: Room | r.suitableFor(c))
pre self.getInstructors() − > **exists** (x: InstructorI | x.suitableFor(c))
post self.getAllCourses() − > includes(c)

The precondition of the method *deleteCourse* requires that the course to be deleted is actually scheduled. The postcondition of this method ensures that the course is not scheduled any more.

context IRegistrar:: deleteCourse(Course c):
pre self.getAllCourses() − > includes(c)
post not (self.getAllCourses() − > includes(c))

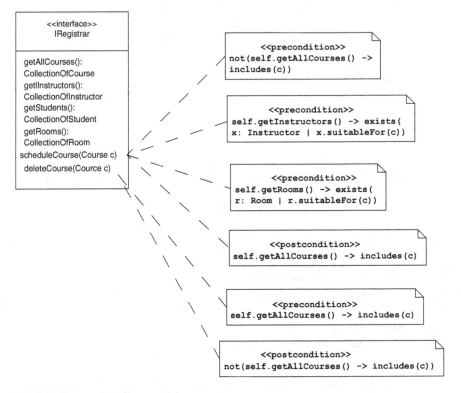

Fig. 4.5 Course scheduling constraints

The above pre and post conditions are specified in a UML diagram given in Fig. 4.5.

The interface *IStudent* has a method *getMyCourses* which represents the one to many relationship of the entity type *Student* and the entity type *Course*. The other such relationship specified by the method *getAllCourses* allows a student to access all scheduled courses. The methods *enrollInCourse* and *dropCourse* specify the corresponding use cases.

interface IStudent {
Collection<Course> getAllCourses();
Collection<Course> getMyCourses();
void enrollInCourse(Course c);
void dropCourse(Course c);
}

The first precondition of the method *enrollInCourse* requires that the student is not already enrolled in the course. The second precondition requires that the set of prerequisites of the course is a subset of the set of courses already taken by the student. The third precondition requires that the course is open for enrollment. The postcondition ensures that the course is in the set of courses taken by the student.

context IStudent:: enrollInCourse(Course c):
pre not (self.getMyCourses() − > includes(c))
pre c.getPrerequsites() − > subset(self.getMyCourses())
pre c.open()
post self.getMyCourses() − > includes(c)

The above assertions are represented in a UML diagram in Fig. 4.6.

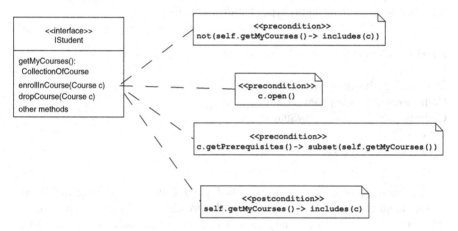

Fig. 4.6 Assertions for enrolling in a course

The precondition of the method *dropCourse* requires that the course to be deleted is in the set of courses taken by the student. The postcondition ensures that it is not anymore.

context IStudent:: dropCourse(Course c):
pre self.getMyCourses() − > includes(c)
post not (self.getMyCourses() − > includes(c))

The above assertions are represented in a UML diagram in Fig. 4.7.

The interface *ICourse* represents the corresponding entity type and contains methods required by the entity types *Registrar* and *Student*. These methods include checking whether the course is open for enrollment, who the instructor is, what the set of prerequisites are, the scheduled time for the course, and the set of students enrolled in the course. The method *getInstructor* specifies one side of the many to one association of the entity types *Course* and *Instructor*. The method *getPrerequisites* represents a many to many association of the entity type *Course*

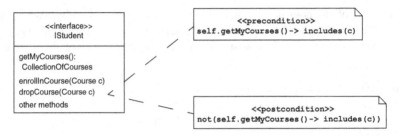

Fig. 4.7 Assertions for dropping a course

with itself. The method *getMyStudents* represents one side of the many to many relationship between the entity types *IStudent* and *ICourse*.

interface ICourse {
boolean open();
InstructorI getInstructor();
Collection<Course> getPrerequisites();
Collection<Student> getMyStudents();
Time getTime();
Room getClassRoom();
}

The interface *InstructorI* has a method *getMyCourses* producing the set of courses taught by the instructor. This method represents one side of the one to many relationship between courses and instructors. A boolean method *suitableFor* which checks whether the instructor is suitable to be scheduled for a particular course.

interface InstructorI {
Collection<Course> getMyCourses();
boolean suitableFor(Course c);
}

The interface *IRoom* has a method *maxCapacity* that specifies the maximum capacity of the room and a method which determines whether the room is suitable for a particular course.

interface IRoom {
boolean suitableFor(Course c);
int maxCapacity();
}

4.2   From Interfaces to Classes

In the UML methodology the structural model of an application environment is
represented as a diagram specifying the relevant entity types and their relationships.
The two orthogonal types of relationships are inheritance and associations. This
diagram is in UML called the class diagram since the entity types are specified as
UML classes (templates with field and method signatures).

The fact that the UML structural model is heavily based on associations has
a decisive impact on mapping that model to code. In our methodology we first
represent entity types as interfaces. Interfaces exist in UML, but are not given the
role that they should have. Representing the structural model in terms of interfaces
provides a level of abstraction in which many details of the actual code as it appears
in classes are still left unspecified.

This first step of mapping to code clearly shows that the representation of the
model will contain multiple collections. This is a consequence of the design methodology that emphasizes associations in addition to inheritance. These collections have
a distinctive property: they have long life times. More specifically, these collections
of objects exist before any particular use case is invoked and continue to exists with
some changes beyond completion of a use case. In other words, these are persistent
collections. Creating and managing persistent collections requires a special software
technology that is the topic of Chap. 5.

4.2.1   Investment Management Application

In the Investment management application that we considered first persistent
collections are a collection of assets, a collection of portfolios, a collection of
investors and a collection of brokers specified below. This is an obvious conclusion
from the interface model and the role that these collections play in that model in
specifying associations.

```
Collection<Asset> assets;
Collection<Portfolio> portfolios;
Collection<Investor> investors;
Collection< Broker> brokers;
```

Not only are the above collections persistent, but so are their elements. So implementation of the Investment management model requires creation and management
of persistent objects of various types, including the collection types. All of this will
be discussed in Chap. 5.

In the specification of the class *Asset* the method *getBrokers* acts on the collection
of all brokers and traverses two associations invoking methods *getMyPortfolios* and
getPortfolioAssets. Representation of this method is still declarative as it makes use
of queries. Queries come naturally with collections, but object-oriented languages
do not have them with one exception to be discussed in Chap. 5.

```
class Asset implements IAsset {
  private float price;
  public getPrice() {
    return this.price;
  }
  public boolean priceOk() {
    return this.price <= getAcceptableValue();
  }
  public void setPrice(float price) {
    this.price = price;
  }
  public Collection<Broker> getBrokers() {
  return (from b in brokers
    where this in b.getMyPortfolios().getPortfolioAssets()
    select b);
  }
// method getPortfolios
}
```

A fundamental observation is that the procedural code is still specified in a
declarative fashion. The reason is that operating on collections naturally leads to
queries. So not only is the representation of the model developed in the design phase
based on persistent collections, but in addition, representing methods that traverse
the associations in the model is naturally expressed by queries.

A procedural representation of the method *getBrokers* given below makes use of
the *foreach* statement which object-oriented languages have. The method *include*
performs simple addition of the argument object to the receiver collection. This
decomposition could be more procedural by using explicit iteration over the
collection of brokers based on the class Iterator.

```
Collection<Broker> getBrokers() {
  Collection<Broker> result;
  for (Broker b: brokers)
    if (b.getMyPortfolios().getPortfolioAssets().contains(this))
    result.include(b);
  return result;
}
```

The class Portfolio contains components of a portfolio object: a collection of stocks and a collection of bonds. The method *getPortfolioAssets* is first specified in a declarative fashion using a query in its body.

```
class Portfolio implements IPortfolio {
  private Investor owner;
  private Broker manager;
  private Collection< Stock > stocks;
  private Collection< Bond > bonds;
  public Broker getBroker() {
      return this.manager;
  }
  public Investor getInvestor() {
      return this.owner;
  }
  public Collection< Stock> getStocks() {
  return stocks;
  }
  public Collection<Bond> getBonds() {
  return bonds;
  }
  public Collection< Asset > getPortfolioAssets() {
  return (from a in assets
      where (Stock)a in this.getStocks()
      or (Bond)a in this.getBonds())
      select a);
  }
}
```

A procedural representation of the method *getPortfolioAssets* given below makes use of the *foreach* statement.

```
Collection<Asset> getPortfolioAssets() {
  Collection<Asset> result;
  for (Asset a: assets)
      if stocks.contains((Stock)a) or
      bonds.contains((Bond)a) )
      result.include(a);
  return result;
  }
```

The above code should be extended with exception handling in case that type casts fail, but we will not elaborate this further. In the class *Investor* the body of the methods *buyAsset* and *sellAsset* representing the corresponding use cases are still left unspecified at this point.

```
class Investor implements InvestorI {
  private Portfolio myPortfolio;
  public Broker getMyBroker() {
      return this.getMyPortfolio().getBroker();
  }
  public Portfolio getMyPortfolio() {
      return this.myPortfolio;
  }
  public Collection<Asset> getAllAssets() {
      return assets;
  }
  public void buyAsset (Asset a) {
      // code
}
  public void sellAsset (Asset a) {
      // code
  }
// . . .
}
```

The method *getMyPortfolios* of the class *Broker* is specified as a query that acts on the collection of all portfolios and selects those that are managed by the receiver broker object.

```
class Broker implements IBroker {
private String brokerId;
private name;
public String getBrokerId() {
    return this.brokerId;
}
public String getBrokerName() {
    return this.name;
}
public Collection<Asset> getAllAssets() {
    return assets;
}
  public Collection<Portfolio> getMyPortfolios() {
  return (from p in portfolios
```

```
      where p.getBroker()= this
      select p);
  }
//. . .
}
```

The procedural decomposition of the method *getMyPortfolios* is specified below using the *foreach* statement.

```
Collection<Portfolio> getMyPortfolios(){
  Collection<Portfolio> result;
  for (Portfolio p: portfolios)
     if (p.getBroker() = this)
     result.include(p)
  return result;
}
```

4.2.2   Course Management Application

We follow the same methodology in developing classes for the course management application. In the interface model we identified persistent collections of courses, students, instructors and rooms. Element types of these collections are specified by the classes *Course, Student, Instructor* and *Room*. There is only one persistent instance of the class *Registrar* specified in this representation, as specified below.

```
  Collection<Course> courses;
  Collection<Student> students;
  Collection<Instructor> instructors;
  Collection<Room> classrooms;
  Registrar r;
```

The class *Course* implementing the interface *ICourse* has the following structure:

```
class Course implements ICourse {
  private String courseId;
  private String name;
  private Instructor taughtBy;
  private Room classroom;
```

```
private Time schedule;
public String getCourseId() {
   return this.courseId;
}
public String getCourseName() {
   return this.name;
}
public String getInstructor() {
   return this.taughtBy;
}
public Room getRoom() {
   return this.classRoom;
}
public Time getTime() {
   return this.schedule;
}
public boolean open() {
   return this.getMyStudents.size() < classRoom.getMaxCapacity();
}
public Collection<Student> getMyStudents() {
return (from s in students
   where this in s.getMyCourses( )
   select s);
}
}
```

The method *getMyStudents* of the class *Course* acts on the collection of all students to select those enrolled in the course which is the receiver object of this method. The procedural representation of the method *getMyStudents* is given below expressed in terms of the *foreach* statement.

```
Collection<Student> getMyStudents() {
private Collection<Student> result;
for (Student s: students)
   if (s.getMyCourses().contains(this))
   result.include(s)
}
```

The method *getMyCourses* of the class *Student* acts on the collection of all courses to select those that have the receiver student object of this method enrolled in a course.

```
class Student implements IStudent {
  String studentId;
  String name;
  String getStudentId() {
     return this.studentId;
  }
  String geStudentName() {
     return this.name;
  }
  public Collection<Course> getAllCourses() {
  return courses;
  }
  pubic Collection<Course> getMyCourses() {
  return (from c in courses
     where this in c.getMyStudents()
     select c);
  }
public void enollInCourse(Course c) {
... }
public void dropCourse(Course c) {
... }
// ...
}
```

The procedural representation of the method *getMyCourses* of the class *Student* makes use of the *foreach* statement.

```
Collection<Course> getMyCourses() {
Collection<Course> result;
 for (Course c: courses)
    if (c.getMyStudents().contains(this))
    result.include(c);
 return result;
}
```

The method *getMyCourses* of the class *Instructor* acts on the collection of courses to select those that are taught by the instructor which is the receiver object of this course.

```
class Instructor implements InstructorI {
 private String name;
 private String suitableFor(Course c) {
    // code
 }
```

```
public Collection<Course> getMyCourses() {
return (from c in courses
    where this = c.getInstructor()
    select c);
 }
// . . .
}
```

The procedural representation of the method *getMyCourses* of the class *Instructor* is given below.

```
Collection<Course> getMyCourses() {
private Collection<Course> result;
 for (Course c: courses)
    if (c.getInstructor()=this)
    result.include(c);
 return result;
}
```

The class *Room* implementing the interface *IRoom* has the following structure:

```
class Room implements IRoom{
 private int maxCapacity;
 private int getMaxCapacity() {;
    return maxCapacity;
    }
 public boolean suitableFor(Course c) {
 //code
 }
}
```

The class *Registrar* implementing the interface *IRegistrar* has the structure given below. The methods *scheduleCourse* and *deleteCourse* representing the corresponding use cases require procedural code which is still left unspecified at this point.

```
class Registrar implements IRegistrar {
 public Collection<Course> getAllCourses() {
 return courses;
 }
 public Collection<Course> getInstructors() {
 return instructors;
 }
```

```
public Collection<Course> getStudents() {
return students;
}
public Collection<Room> getRooms() {
return rooms;
}
public void scheduleCourse(Course c) {
    // code
}
public void deleteCourse(Course c) {
    // code
}
// . . .
}
```

4.3 Model and Code Management

A model that has been designed and implemented will typically require changes over time that would reflect changes in the application environment.

4.3.1 Forward Engineering

The term forward engineering refers to the design and implementation of a model of an application environment. For example, assume that the result of design is the following model with two entity types *Asset* and *Portfolio* and their many to many relationship (Fig. 4.8).

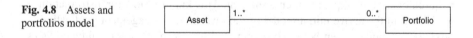

Fig. 4.8 Assets and portfolios model

This model could be implemented by the code whose general structure is specified as follows.

```
class InvestmentManagement {
 Collection<Asset> assets;
 Collection<Portfolio> portfolios;
 interface IAsset
 { . . . }
 interface IPortfolio
 { . . . }
 class Asset implements IAsset
```

```
{ ... }
class Portfolio implements IPortfolio
{ ... }
// ...
}
```

In the interfaces *IAsset* and *IPortfolio* given below methods *getPortfolios* and *getAssets* implement the many to many association between entity types *Asset* and *Portfolio*.

```
interface IAsset {
  String getName();
  String getCode();
  Collection <Portfolio> getPortfolios();
}
```

```
interface IPortfolio {
  float getTotalValue();
  Collection <Asset> getAssets();
}
```

4.3.2 Model Transformation

Among possible transformations of an object-oriented model those that are based on inheritance are in fact in the core of the object-oriented paradigm and require the least amount of reengineering effort. These transformations amount to extending the existing model by introducing their subtypes to reflect the evolution of the requirements of an application environment. This kind of model transformation is performed in the above initial model of the investment management application to produce the model given below. In this model transformation two subtypes *Stock* and *Bond* of the entity type *Asset* are introduced.

4.3.3 Refactoring

The term refactoring refers to producing new code from the existing code. In our example we rely on inheritance. New code is produced by inheritance. The class *ExtendedInvestmentManagement* is derived by inheritance from the class *InvestmentManagement* by introducing new subtypes *Stock* and *Bond* of the type *Asset* (Fig. 4.9).

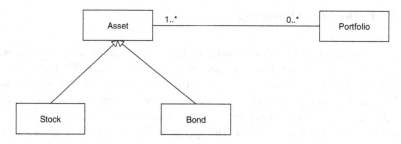

Fig. 4.9   Extended assets and portfolios model

```
class ExtendedInvestmentManagement extends InvestmentManagement {
  interface IStock extends IAsset
  { float getShareValue();
  }
  interface IBond extends IAsset
  { float getYield();
  }
  class Stock implements IStock
  { ... }
  class Bond implements IAsset
  { ... }
}
```

4.3.4   Model Transformation

A different type of model transformation is actually required if we want to implement the produced object-oriented model using object-relational technology. This technology is typically used to manage data of an application environment. The transformation that reflects the requirements of the object-relational model amounts to representing the many to many relationship in terms of two many to one relationships as in the figure below (Fig. 4.10).

Fig. 4.10   Toward relational representation

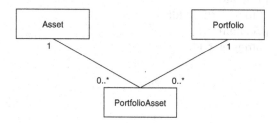

4.3.5 Forward Engineering

An implementation of the above model in the object-relational technology will include three tables *Asset*, *Portfolio*, and *PortfolioAsset* where the table *PortfolioAsset* represents the many to many association between entity types *Asset* and *Portfolio*. In the relational model each table will be equipped with a key which uniquely identifies a tuple of a relation. This representation is specified below in the notation of LINQ to SQL of C#. The special attribute [Table] specifies that the underlying class corresponds to a database table. The attribute [Column] specifies that the field that it annotates in fact represents a column of the underlying database table. The annotation [IsPrimaryKey=true] specifies a field that in fact represents the primary key of the underlying table. All of this will be further elaborated in Chap. 5.

```
[Table]
class Asset {
[Column] [IsPrimaryKey=true]
  String assetId;
[Column]
  String name;
}
```

```
[Table]
class Portfolio {
[Column] [IsPrimaryKey=true]
  String portfolioId;
[Column]
  float totalValue;
}
```

Elements of the table *PortfolioAsset* are pairs consisting of an asset key and a portfolio key.

```
[Table]
class PortfolioAsset {
[Column]
  String portfolioId;
[Column]
  String assetId;
}
```

4.3.6 *Refactoring*

Changing the original object-oriented code to reflect the object-relational model is
nontrivial. The structure of the new code has the following code in which *Table* is a
parametric class developed to fit the requirements of the relational model.

```
class InvestmentManagement {
  Table<Asset> assets;
  Table<Portfolio> portfolios;
  Table<PortfolioAsset> portfolioAssets;
  interface IAsset
  { ... }
  interface IPortfolio
  { ... }
  interface IPortfolioAsset
  { ... }
  class Asset implements IAsset
  { ... }
  class Portfolio implements IPortfolio
  { ... }
  class PortfolioAsset implements IPortfolioAsset
  { ... }
}
```

In the class *Asset* given below of particular interest is the method *getPortfolios*.
This method requires traversal of the table *PortfolioAsset* and matching the asset id
in the table *Asset* with the asset id in the table *PortfolioAsset*. This is a very basic
implementation of the relational operation called join.

```
class Asset implements IAsset {
  String assetId;
  String name;
  String getAssetId() {
  return assetId;
  }
  String getName() {
  return name;
  }
  Asset getAsset(String assetId)
  { return (from a in assets
      where a.assetId = assetId
      select a);
  }
```

```
Table<Portfolio> getPortfolios()
{ Table<Portfolio> result;
  for (PortfolioAsset pA: portfolioAssets)
    if (pA.assetId = this.assetId)
    result.include(getPortfolio(pA.portfolioId));
  return result;
}
```

Likewise, in the class *Portfolio* given below of particular interest is the method *getAssets*. This method requires traversal of the table *PortfolioAsset* and matching the portfolio id in the table Portfolio with the portfolio id in the table *PortfolioAsset*.

```
class Portfolio implements IPortfolio {
  String portfolioId;
  float totalValue;
  String getPortfolioId() {
  return portfolioId;
  }
  Float getTotalValue() {
  return totalValue;
  }
  Portfolio getPortfolio(String portfolioId) {
  { if (this.portfolioId = portfolioId) return this
    else return null;
  }
```

```
Table<Portfolio> getAssets()
{ Table<Asset> result;
  for (PortfolioAsset pA: portfolioAssets)
    if (pA.portfolioId = this.portfolioId)
    result.include(getAsset(pA.assetId));
  return result;
}
```

4.3.7 *Reverse Engineering*

The term reverse engineering refers to a process in which the starting point is the existing code and the model is not necessarily available. If in our example all we have is the object-relational code given above, a correct methodology would require reconstructing a model from the code. From that point one may transform the model to the object-oriented model and produce the corresponding code by forward engineering.

The above discussed types of model and code transformation are shown in Fig. 4.11.

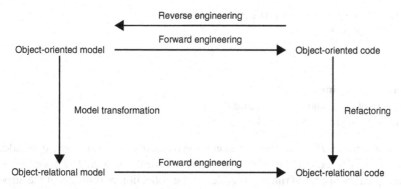

Fig. 4.11   Model and code transformations

4.4   Interplay of Inheritance and Constraints

Interplay between constraints and inheritance is nontrivial and OCL specifications do not address these subtleties. Consider an airport model which consists of two entity types *Airport* and *Runway* with many to one association between runways and airports. Inheritance appears in this model if we consider two types of airports: domestic and international, as in Fig. 4.12.

An airport is associated with a number of runways (at least one) and a runway belongs to a single airport. The invariant of the class *Airport* specifies that the number of runways must be greater than zero and less than 30.

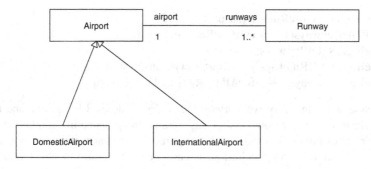

Fig. 4.12   Airports and runways

```
interface IAirport {
 int getNoOfRunways();
 Collection<Runway> getRunways();
 void addRunway(Runway strip);
 void closeRunway(Runway strip);
 // other methods
}
```

```
interface InternationalAirportI extends IAirport {
// additional methods
}
```

context Airport **inv**
  self.getNoOfRunways() >= 1 **and**
  self.getNoOfRunways() <= 30

The method *addRunway* has a precondition requiring that the runway to be added does not already exist in the collection of runways of the airport. The postcondition ensures that the specified runway is added to the collection of runways of the airport following the association link *runways*.

context Airport:: addRunway(strip: Runway)
pre not (self.getRunways() − > **exists**(r: Runway | r=strip))
post self.getRunways() − > **exists**(r: Runway | r=strip)

The method *closeRunway* of the class *Airport* has a precondition that the runway to be closed exists in the collection of the runways of the airport. There are several postconditions. The first postcondition ensures that the airport still has at least one runway. The second postcondition ensures that the number of runways of the airport was reduced by one. The third postcondition ensures that the closed runway does not exist in the collection of runways of the airport.

context Airport:: closeRunway(strip: Runway)
  pre self.getRunways() − > **exists**(r:Runway | r=strip)
  post self.getNoOfRunways() >= 1
  post self.getNoOfRunways() = self.getNoOfRunways()@**pre** -1
  post self.getRunways() − >**forAll** (r: Runway | r <> strip)

Consider now an entity type *InternationalAirport* derived by inheritance from the interface *Airport*. The invariant of this class is strengthened in comparison with the invariant of the class *Airport* and it requires that an international airport must have ten or more runways. In addition, at least one of them must be an international airport as specified in the second invariant.

context InternationalAirport **inv**
  self.getNOfRunways() >= 10
  self.getRunways() − > **exists** (r: Runway | r.international=true)

Consider now the method *closeRunway* of the class *InternationalAirport*. This method is inherited from the class *Airport* and it is redefined. Its postcondition strengthens the postcondition of the inherited method. The number of runways is required to be greater than or equal to 10 and at least one of the remaining runways must be an international one.

One would want to strengthen the precondition of the redefined method *closeRunway* to require that the runway to be closed is not the only international runway, but this is not possible. The precondition of the inherited method is required to be the same as in the class *Airport*.

context InternationalAirport:: closeRunway(strip: Runway)
post self.getNoOfRunways() >= 10
post self.getRunways() − > **exists** (r: Runway | r.international=true)

UML diagram in Fig. 4.13 illustrates the above situation.

4.5 Models with Complex Constraints

In this section we specify the interfaces and the associated constraints for the flight management model given in Fig. 4.14. This is an example of a complex application with elaborate constraints.

The interface for the entity type *Flight* is given below. A flight has a flight id, origin and destination of type *Airport*, departure time and arrival time, and an aircraft assigned to the flight.

interface IFlight {
  String getFlightId();
  Airport getOrigin();
  Airport getDestination();
  Time getDepartureTime();
  Time getArrivalTime();
  String getFlightStatus();
  Aircraft getAircraft();
}

The invariant of the entity type *Flight* given below guarantees that the origin and the destination of a flight are different and that the departure time precedes the arrival time. If the departure time is less than the current time, the flight status is idle. If the departure time is less than the arrival time the flight status is either takeoff, flying or landing.

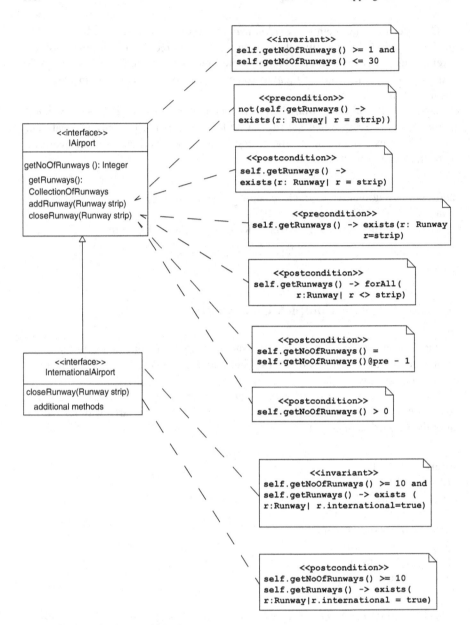

Fig. 4.13 Specifications and inheritance

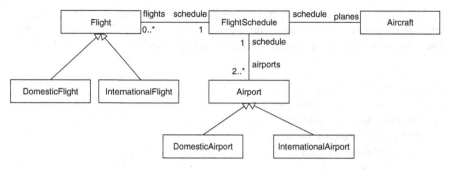

Fig. 4.14 Flight management relationships

context IFlight **inv**
  self.getOrigin() <> self.getDestination()
  self.getDepartureTime() < self.getArrivalTime()
  Time::now() < self.getDepartureTime() **implies** self.getFlightStatus() ="idle"
  Time::now() > self.getDepartureTime() **and** Time::now()
  <= self.getArrivalTime()
implies (self.getFlightStatus()="takeoff" **or**
    self.getFlightStatus() = "flying" **or** self.getFlightStatus()="landing")

  The above invariants are specified in a UML like diagram given in Fig. 4.15.

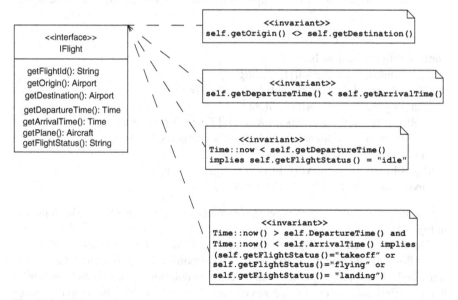

Fig. 4.15 Flight invariants

The interface for the entity type *FlightSchedule* is given below. A flight schedule consists of a collection of flights and a collection of airports. The methods of this interface allow scheduling a flight, cancelling a flight, and redirecting a flight.

```
interface IFlightSchedule {
  Collection<Flight> getFlights();
  Collection<Airport> getAirports();
  Collection<Aircraft> getAircraft();
  void scheduleFlight(Flight f);
  void cancelFlight(String flightId);
  void redirectFlight(String flightId; Airport newDestination);
}
```

The invariants of the class *FlightSchedule* specify that the *flightId* is a key in the collection of flights associated with the flight schedule. This invariant requires traversal of the association *flights*. It says that if the flight ids of two flights are the same, then these flights are in fact equal. In order to specify this invariant, the universal quantifier **forAll** is required.

The next invariant specifies a referential integrity constraint. It requires that all references to airplanes in the flight schedule indeed refer to aircraft existing in the collection of aircraft as specified by the association planes. This constraint requires both the universal and existential quantifiers.

The third and the fourth invariants are similar referential constraints that apply to references to airports in the flight schedule as specified by the association *airports*.

context IFlightSchedule **inv**
  self.getFlights() − > **forAll**(f1, f2: Flight |
      f1.getFlightId() = f2.getFlightId() **implies** f1=f2)
  self.getFlights() − > **forAll** (f: Flight |
      self.getPlanes() − > **exists** (a: Aircraft | f.getAircraft() = a))
  self.getFlights() − > **forAll**(f: Flight | self.getAirports() − >
      exists (a: Airport | f.getOrigin() = a))
  self.getFlights() − > **forAll**(f: Flight | self.getAirports() |
      exists (a: Airport | f.getDestination()= a))

The invariants of the entity type *FlightSchedule* are given in a UML like diagram in Fig. 4.16.

The method *scheduleFlight* of the interface *IFlightSchedule* takes as its arguments flight id, the origin and the destination airports, the departure and the arrival time, and the aircraft to be scheduled. The precondition of this method requires that the origin and the destination airports are different and that the departure time precedes the arrival time. In addition, the third precondition requires that the flight is not already scheduled. The fourth precondition requires that the aircraft to be

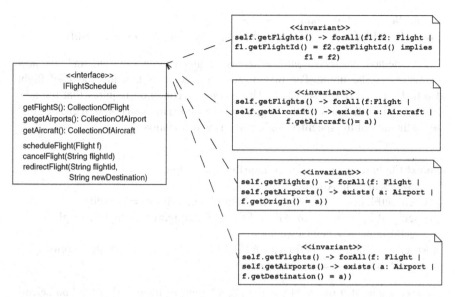

Fig. 4.16 Flight schedule invariants

scheduled indeed exists in the collection of all aircraft associated with the flight schedule. The postcondition guarantees that the flight is indeed scheduled, i.e., it exists in the flight schedule.

context FlightSchedule :: scheduleFlight(
    flightId: String,
    to, from :Airport,
    departureTime, arrivalTime : DateTime,
    plane: Aircraft)
pre to <> from
pre departureTime < arrivalTime
pre this.getFlights() − > **forAll** (f: Flight | f.getFlightId() <> flightId())
pre this.getPlanes() − > **exists** (a: Aircraft | a=plane)
post self.getFlights() − > **exists** (f: Flight | f.getFlightId() = flightId)

The method *cancelFlight* of the class *FlightSchedule* has a precondition that requires that the flight to be canceled exists in the flight schedule. The second precondition requires that the status of the flight to be cancelled is not landing. The postcondition ensures that the cancelled flight is not in the schedule any more.

context FlightSchedule :: cancelFlight(flightId: String)
  pre self.getFlights() − > **exists** (f: Flight | f.getFlightId() = flightId)
  pre self.getFlights() − > **exists** (f: Flight | f.getFlightId() = flightId

implies f.getFlightStatus() <> "landing")
post self.getFlights() − > **forAll** (f: Flight | f.getFlightId() <> flightId)

The method *redirectFlight* has as its arguments the flight id and the new destination of the flight. The first precondition requires that the specified flight id actually exists in the schedule. The second precondition requires that the new destination is different from the original destination. The postcondition ensures that the destination of the specified flight is the new destination.

context FlightSchedule::redirectFlight(flightId: String,
    newDestination: Airport)
pre self.getFlights() − > **exists** (f: Flight | f.getFlightId() = flightId)
pre self.getFlights() − > **forAll** (f: Flight | f.getFlightId() = flightId **implies**
    f.getOrigin() <> newDestination)
post self.getFlights() − > **forAll** (f: Flight | f.getFlightI() = flightId **implies**
    f.getDestination() =newDestination)

An example of a query method is *flightDepartureWithin*. This method selects a set of flights with the departure time within a specified time interval. The first precondition requires that the specified interval is not empty and that the end of the interval is greater than the current time. The postcondition specifies the result of the query denoted by the keyword *result*. The result contains flights with the departure time in the specified interval.

context FlightSchedule :: flightDepartureWithin (
beginTime, endTime: DateTime): Set(Flight)
pre beginTime < endTime
pre endTime > DateTime::now()
post result− > **forAll** (f: Flight |
    f.getDepartureTime() >= beginTime **and** f.getArrivalTime() <= endTime)

4.6 Exercises

1. Specify the code for the class *Flight* that implements the interface *IFlight* so that constraints specified for the interface *IFlight* will be satisfied.
2. Specify the code for the class *FlightSchedule* that implements the interface *IFlightSchedule* in such a way that all constraints specified for the interface *IFlightSchedule* will be satisfied.
3. Specify the interfaces for the Reservation subsystem of the Flight management system with the required constraints such as those for the methods *makeReservation* and *cancelReservation*.

4. Specify the code for the classes implementing the interfaces of the reservation subsystem of the Flight management application in such a way that the constraints specified for those interfaces are satisfied.

5. Refactor the implementation of the Flight management system extending the model with inheritance as follows: *Flight* has two subtypes *DomesticFlight* and *InternationalFlight* and *Airport* has two subtypes *InternationalAirport* and *DomesticAirport*.

6. The model of Flight management system is actually object-relational in many ways. There are three collections (relations) of flights, airports and aircraft and the flight schedule represents their ternary relationship specified by keys. Transform this model into a true object-oriented model and refactor the code.

7. Refactor the code implementing the Course management model assuming that the initial model without inheritance is extended with subtypes as in Fig. 4.4.

8. Transform the object-oriented model of the Course management application into an object-relational model and refactor the code accordingly.

9. Specify the constraints of the subclasses *Undergraduate* and *Graduate* of the class *Student* of the Course management application that makes the constraints of these two subtypes compatible with the constraints of the class *Student*. Implement these two subclasses in such a way that the specified constraints are satisfied.

Chapter 5
Data Management

Assume that a model is designed as a collection of interrelated entity types with association and inheritance relationships along with use cases. Consider now the lifetimes of instances of the entity types in the model.

Objects (instances of entity types) that have long lifetimes that extend beyond activations of use cases are called persistent objects. By way of comparison, during activation of a use case, objects whose lifetime does not extend that activation may be created. Such objects are called transient objects. Managing persistent objects in addition to managing transient objects is a major technical issue and requires a special software technology to be elaborated in this chapter.

A use case is implemented as a sequence of actions on persistent and transient objects. In UML such a sequence is specified by the sequence diagram of a use case. This sequence should have special properties which make such a sequence a transaction. Basically, the notion of a transaction allows a sequence of actions representing a use case to be considered as a logical unit. In this chapter we define more precisely properties of use cases viewed as transactions and we describe a software technology that is needed in order to implement use cases so that these properties are satisfied.

5.1 Implementing Use Cases

Consider now two critical and related technical issues in implementing uses cases. We will look again at the use cases *BuyAsset* and *SellAsset* of the investment management application.

Use case: BuyAsset

Entities: Investor, Asset, Portfolio, Broker

Actors: Investor, Broker

© Springer International Publishing AG 2017
S. Alagić, *Software Engineering: Specification, Implementation, Verification,*
DOI 10.1007/978-3-319-61518-9_5

Constraints:

Preconditions: assetPriceOK, brokerApproves

PostCondition: assetInPortfolio

Frame: All other assets in portfolio unaffected

Use case: SellAsset

Entities: Investor, Asset, Portfolio, Broker

Actors: Investor, Broker

Preconditions: assetInPortfolio, brokerApproves

Postcondition: not assetInPortfolio

Frame: All other assets in portfolio unaffected

Entity types *Investor*, *Asset*, *Portfolio*, and *Broker* have a distinctive property. Instances of these entity types, and in fact their collections, have long lifetimes. They existed (were created) before these use cases are activated and they continue to exist (unless explicitly destroyed by a use case) beyond activation of these use cases. In fact, we have collections of these instances that have this property. Those are: a collection of investors, a collection of assets, a collection of portfolios and a collection of brokers. A sequence diagram for the use cases *BuyAsset* and *SellAsset* shows that these use cases are implemented as sequences of messages. In our view, each such sequence should have the following properties:

– *Atomicity*

A use case is executed completely as a unit. Partial executions caused by errors and other failures are unacceptable. If they happen, they will have no impact on the entities involved in the use case. That is, a use case is executed completely, or else it will have no effect at all. This property is called atomicity.

– *Consistency*

The second property is that an implementation of a use case must satisfy all the constraints associated with a use case. This means the preconditions, the postconditions, and the frame constraints of the use case, as well as constraints associated with each entity type involved in the use case, such as class invariants, and preconditions and postconditions of methods used in the implementation of the use case. This property is called consistency.

– *Isolation*

The third property is related to the fact that multiple use cases are activated and executed concurrently. In this particular case, multiple investors are concurrently buying and selling assets. An obvious requirement is that individual activations of a use case should not be affected by concurrently executed use cases. This property is called isolation.

– *Durability*

Finally, if a use case is successfully (and hence completely) executed, the effect of this execution will persist. In this particular example, purchases and sales of assets will persist beyond executions of the corresponding use cases. This property is called durability.

The above four properties are properties of ACID transactions. The above informal analysis shows that use cases should be implemented as transactions that act on persistent objects.

5.2 Persistence

A persistent object is an object whose lifetime extends beyond execution of the program that created that object. Persistent objects are thus objects with possibly very long lifetimes. This concept is implemented by providing some form of a persistent store containing objects that are promoted to persistence.

Among a variety of models of persistence the model of *orthogonal persistence* deserves special attention. This model has the following properties:

– *Orthogonality*

Persistence is independent of types, i.e., an object (or a value) of any type may be persistent.
– *Transitivity (reachability)*

If an object is promoted to persistence, so are all of its components, direct or indirect.
– *Transparency*

The details of the persistence supporting architecture are completely hidden from the users.

Widely used technologies typically support only some of the above properties. For example, in relational systems only objects of type relation are persistent. Even tuples can persist only as long as they appear in relations, not by themselves. In Java, only objects of classes that implement a special interface *Serializable* can persist. In relational systems transparency is supported. In Java, a user must deal with opening and closing files, writing objects to files and reading objects from files. Basic relational systems do not have complex objects per se. Java supports transitivity, with some issues to be explained in this section.

The main issues related to persistence will be illustrated using the following classes.

```
public class Aircraft
{ private String model;
  private Pilot pilot;
  public Aircraft(String aModel)
  { model = aModel; pilot = null; }
```

```
public assignPilot(Pilot p)
{ pilot=p;}
// other methods
}


public class Pilot
{ private String name;
  private int points;
  public Pilot(String pName, int pPoints)
  { name = pName; points = pPoints; }
// other methods
}
```

The transparency property hides non-trivial complexity of the underlying persistence architecture. This is illustrated in Fig. 5.1.

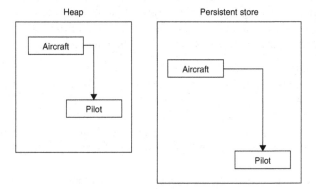

Fig. 5.1 Persistent complex objects

Heap is a main memory area where objects are created. Persistent store is an external memory (like disc) that holds persistent objects. The structure of the aircraft object is represented on the heap using pointers that are in fact heap addresses. So an aircraft object will contain a pointer to a pilot object on the heap. When a complex object is promoted to persistence, its structure must be maintained. However, the pointers in the persistent store (typically disc addresses) are different from the heap pointers. This means that the whole complex object structure of an object must be preserved in the persistent store, and pointers to component objects must be implemented as disc addresses. This procedure is called swizzelling out. The reverse operation is swizzelling in. It restores the complete persistent object structure on the heap. In a transparent model of persistence these procedures are automatic and completely hidden from the users.

One implication of transitivity is that if an object is promoted to persistence, its class object should also be promoted to persistence. The reason is that an object contains a reference to its class object. In addition, in order to perform actions on complex objects, one needs to know what types of objects are in the persistent store.

5.3 File-Based Persistence

The Java model of persistence offers transitivity, but not transparency nor orthogonality. Only objects of types that implement a special interface *Serializable* could be made persistent. This leads to a paradox: it is not possible to define a persistent collection whose elements are of the type *Object*, because *Object* does not implement *Serializable*. That would have to be the case in order for the Java model of persistence to be orthogonal.

The Java model does not satisfy the transparency requirement because it is based on the file system, so users have to open and close files, read and write objects from and to files, etc. However, transitivity is supported to the extent that it is possible to write a complete complex object to a file with a single statement, and read a complex object from a file in a single statement. This is accomplished through interfaces *ObjectInput* and *ObjectOutput* and their implementing classes. These interfaces also have methods for reading and writing values of simple types that are specified in the Java interfaces *DataInput* and *DataOutput*.

The method *writeObject* takes an object of any type and writes it to the output file stream. The underlying algorithm represents the structure of a complex object as a sequence of bytes, hence the term serialization. This is illustrated in Fig. 5.2.

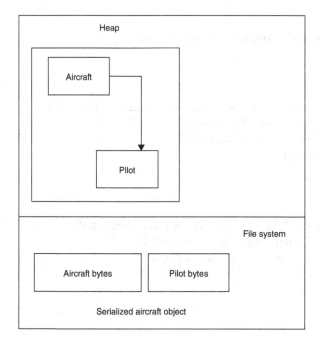

Fig. 5.2 Serialized complex object

```
public interface ObjectOutput extends DataOutput
{
  void writeObject(Object obj);
      throws IOexception;
  // other methods
}
```

The method *readObject* reads an object from a file input stream. The complex object structure is restored on the heap based on its serialized representation.

```
public interface ObjectInput extends DataInput
{
  Object readObject()
      throws ClassNotFoundException, IOexception;
  // other methods
  }
```

The argument of the method *writeObject* is necessarily of type *Object* and the result of the method *readObject* is necessarily of type *Object* as well. This reflects the requirement that objects of any type may be read or written. This means that a type cast is necessary when reading an object in order to perform specific actions on the object read. This dynamic check is unavoidable. In general, an object is written by one program and read by a different program. The type cast verifies that the type assumption made by the second program is in fact correct. This is illustrated in the following code:

```
public class Aircraft implements Serializable {
// . . .
}


FileOutputStream fileOut = new FileOutputStream("AircraftFile");
ObjectOutput out = new ObjectOutputStream(fileOut);
aircraftObj = new Aircraft("Boeing777");
out.writeObject(aircraftObj);
out.flush();
out.close();


FileInputStream fileIn = new FileInputStream("AircraftFile");
ObjectInput in = new ObjectInputStream(fileIn);
Aircraft aircraftObj= (Aircraft) in.readObject();
in.close();
```

In the Java model of persistence, class objects are not written to the file streams. Strictly speaking, this means that the model does not fully support transitivity. Java uses a shortcut to store the class type information using a hashed value that is subsequently used in a type cast to verify its type correctness.

5.4 Transactions

The Java model of persistence has several limitations. Since we are looking at techniques for implementing use cases, a particularly important limitation is lack of support for transactions. In this chapter we consider two of the available persistent technologies that provide support for transactions.

The JDO (Java Data Objects) model of persistence is not orthogonal. It is based on the notion of persistent capable classes. Only objects of persistent capable classes can persist. A persistence capable class is declared as follows:

```
@PersistenceCapable
public class Aircraft
{ . . .
{
```

In addition, if objects of a class manipulate persistent objects, such a class must be declared as persistent aware.

JDO has the notion of persistent manager which controls actions on persistent objects in a collection of persistent objects associated with a particular persistent manager. A persistent manager is declared as follows:

```
PersistentManagerFactory pmf = get persistent manager factory;
PersistentManager pm = pmf.getPersistentManager();
```

In order to make an object persistent, the method *makePersistent* of the class *PersistentManager* is invoked. So promoting an object *a* to persistence is accomplished by the following statement.

```
pm.makePersistent(a)
```

The basic actions of the class *Transaction* are *begin, commit* and *rollback*. A persistent manager keeps track of the currently executed transaction. An example of such a transaction is given below. Tx.begin() starts the transaction. An aircraft object is then created and promoted to persistence. If there are no exceptions, the transaction is committed by the statement Tx.commit() and its effects persist. Otherwise, exceptions are handled. Finally, if the transaction has not been successfully committed, its effects are rolled back executing the statement Tx.rollBack().

```
Transaction Tx = pm.currentTransaction();
try
{Tx.begin();
 // transaction code
 Tx.commit();
}
catch (Exception ex)
 { exception handling }
finally
{     if (Tx.isActive())
      Tx.rollback();
}
 pm.close();
}
```

JDO has the notion of the extent of a persistent capable class. The extent of a class is the collection of all objects of that class. A persistent capable class maintains this collection through its persistent manager. Getting access to the extent of a class *Aircraft* is accomplished by the following statement:

```
Extent e = pm.getExtent(Aircraft.class)
```

Notice that this statement refers to the class object. JDO supports reachability or transitive persistence. When an object is promoted to persistence, all objects that it refers to directly or indirectly are promoted to persistence as in the sample transaction given below. So making an aircraft object persistent will also make its associated pilot object persistent.


```
Transaction Tx = pm.currentTransaction();
try
{Tx.begin();
 Aircraft a= new Aircraft("Boeing 777");
 pm.makePersistent(a);
 Tx.commit();
}
catch (Exception ex)
 { exception handling }
finally
{     if (Tx.isActive())
      Tx.rollback();
}
 pm.close();
}
```

Accessing persistent objects is accomplished by searching the extent of their class. A sample transaction given below creates an iterator over the extent of the class *Aircraft* and displays the pilot of each aircraft in the extent.

```
Transaction Tx = pm.currentTransaction();
try
{
 Tx.begin();
 Extent e = pm.getExtent(Aircraft.class);
 Iterator it = e.iterator();
 while (it.hasNext());
 { Aircraft a = (Aircraft)it.next();
 a.pilot.display();
 }
 Tx.commit();
}
catch (Exception ex)
 { exception handling }
finally
{if (Tx.isActive())
 Tx.rollback();
}
 pm.close();
}
```

The above example is written in the spirit of JDO where parametric types are not used. It shows how important those types are for persistent collections. If the dynamic type check caused by the type cast (Aircraft)it.next() fails, so will the transaction unless this error is handled successfully.

Updating a persistent object requires a search of the extent of its class to locate that object, as in a sample transaction given below. This transaction assigns a new pilot to aircraft objects of a particular aircraft model.

```
Transaction Tx = pm.currentTransaction();
try
{
 Tx.begin();
 Extent e = pm.getExtent(Aircraft.class);
 Iterator it = e.iterator();
 while (it.hasNext());
 { Aircraft a = (Aircraft)it.next();
 Pilot p = get pilot;
 if (a.model = "Boeing 777")
     a.assignPilot(p);
```

```
}
Tx.commit();
}
catch (Exception ex)
 { exception handling }
finally
{if (Tx.isActive())
 Tx.rollback();
}
 pm.close();
}
```

The method *deletePersistent* of the class *PersistentManager* deletes a persistent object from the persistent store, as in the statement that deletes an aircraft object a:

```
pm.deletePersistent(a)
```

This type of statement appears in the delete transaction given below. The aircraft objects of a particular make are first located and then their pilots are deleted.

```
Transaction Tx = pm.currentTransaction();
try
{
 Tx.begin();
 Extent e = pm.getExtent(Aircraft.class);
 Iterator it = e.iterator();
 while (it.hasNext();
 { Aircraft a = (Aircraft)it.next();
 if (a.model = "Boeing") ;
 pm.deletePersistent(a.pilot);
 Tx.commit();
 }
catch (Exception ex)
 { exception handling }
finally
{if (Tx.isActive())
 Tx.rollback();
}
 pm.close();
}
```

When a persistent object is deleted, the objects that it refers to may also be deleted. This is called cascade deletion because it propagates all the way following object references to immediate and indirect components of the deleted object. Sometimes that is not a correct procedure. For example, deleting an aircraft object does not necessarily mean that the associated pilot object should be deleted. Pilots may exist independently of particular aircraft. Systems like JDO allow selection of the delete procedure by a special parameter.

5.5 Object-Relational Technology

JDO manages objects in the persistent store. The prevailing object-relational database technology manages persistent relations, i.e., flat tables. Because of this, using object-relational technology requires mapping of the object-oriented model developed in the design phase to its relational representation as a collection of flat tables. This mapping comes with nontrivial problems as the object-oriented and the relational models are so very different. On the positive side, object-relational systems offer features of database systems such as concurrent transactions and queries.

In Java Persistence API persistent capable classes are called entity classes. An entity aircraft class is declared as follows:

```
@Entity
public class Aircraft
{ ...
}
```

Object-relational systems have explicit support for user-defined identifiers called primary keys. A primary key determines a unique object of an entity class. In the example below *aircraftId* is declared as the primary key of the class *Aircraft*.

```
@Entity
public abstract class Aircraft
{
  @Id
  protected String aircraftId;
...
}
```

Unlike system-managed object identities in object-oriented systems, this identifier is based on the values of attributes of an object and must be properly managed by the persistent manager to guarantee uniqueness.

An example of inheritance as it applies to entity classes is given below. Entity classes *PasssengerPlane* and *CargoPlane* are derived by inheritance from the abstract entity class *Aircraft*.

```
@Entity
public class PassengerPlane extends Aircraft
{
 int capacity;
...
}
```

```
@Entity
public class CargoPlane extends Aircraft
{
 float maxLoad;
...
}
```

Java persistence API also has the notion of an entity manager associated with a persistent context which is a collection of entity classes and their persistent objects. A persistent manager is declared as follows:

```
@PersistentContext
EntityManager em;
```

A user transaction is declared as a resource as follows:

```
@Resource
UserTransaction Tx;
```

Objects are accessed using the method *find* of the class *EntityManager*. This search is based on the primary key, as in the example below:

```
@PersistentContext
EntityManager em;
public void findAircraft(String id)
{
 Aircraft a = em.find(Aircraft.class, id);
 a.getPilot().display();
}
```

Making an object persistent is accomplished by invoking the method *persist* of the class *EntityManager* as in the example below. An aircraft object is created and then made persistent in the specified persistent context.

```
@PersistentContext
EntityManager em;
public void newAircraft(String id, String model)
{
  Aircraft a = new Aircraft("US1", "Boeing747");
  em.persist(a);
}
```

Deleting a persistent object is accomplished by invoking the method *remove* of the class *EntityManager*, as in the example below. Whether the deletion will be cascaded to immediate and indirect components or not is determined by a parameter which we do not show.

```
@PersistentContext
EntityManager em;
public void removeAircraft(String id)
{
  Aircraft a = em.find(id);
  em.remove(a);
}
```

5.6 Representing Associations

Modeling an application environment as a collection of entities and their relationships was actually introduced in the entity-relationship data model. This is why object-relational systems pay special attention to relationships as they have a well-established relational representation. The relationships are represented in object-oriented systems combining relational features such as keys and foreign keys and object-oriented features such as methods. These techniques are illustrated below as they appear in Java Persistence API for the investment management application.

The relationship between entity types *Investor* and *Portfolio* is one to one. That is, an investor has a unique portfolio and a portfolio has a unique owner. This binary relationship is represented by annotating the method *getPortfolio* of the class *Investor* by the special attribute *OneToOne*. This method returns the portfolio of an investor.

```
public class Investor
{ ...
@OneToOne
public Portfolio getPortfolio() {
      return myPortfolio;
}
```

The inverse relationship is specified in the same manner annotating the method *getOwner* of the class *Portfolio*. This method returns the investor who is the owner of a portfolio.

```
public class Portfolio
{ ...
@OneToOne
public Investor getOwner() {
     return owner;
}
```

The relationship between entity types *Portfolio* and *Broker* is many to one. That is, a portfolio has a unique broker and a broker manages a number of portfolios. So the method *getBroker* of the class *Portfolio* which returns the broker of a portfolio is annotated with the attribute *ManyToOne*.

```
public class Portfolio
{ ...
@ManyToOne
public Broker getBroker() {
     return manager;}
}
```

The method *getMyPortfolios* of the class *Broker* returns a collection of portfolios managed by that broker and it is annotated by the attribute *OneToMany*.

```
public class Broker
{ ...
@OneToMany
public Collection<Portfolio> getMyPortfolios() {
     // select portfolios of this broker;
}
}
```

The relationship between entity types *Asset* and *Portfolio* is many to many. An asset is associated with many portfolios and a portfolio is associated with many assets. This is why the method *getPortfolios* of the class *Asset* is annotated with the attribute *ManyToMany*.

```
public class Asset
{ ...
@ManyToMany
public Collection<Portfolio> getMyPortfolios() {
```

```
    select portfolios having this asset;}
}
```

Likewise, the method *getPortfolioAssets* of the class Portfolio is also annotated with the attribute *ManyToMany*.

```
public class Portfolio
{ . . .
@ManyToMany
public Collection<Asset> getPortfolioAssets() {
    select assets of this portfolio;}
}
```

5.7 Relational Representation

The above described technique of representing relationships among entity types using annotated methods is based on what Java Persistence API does. But in this technology the underlying representation of entity types is relational. We will explain what that representation involves using object-oriented notation which amounts to classes having only simple types of attributes.

The one to one relationship between an investor and a portfolio is represented by the *Investor* class having a field that refers to the primary key of portfolio and the *Portfolio* class has a field that refers to the primary key of the investor. These fields are called foreign keys.

```
public class Investor {
@Id
String investorId;
String portfolioId; // foreign key

. . .
}
```

UML has the notion of a table which allows specification of attributes of such a table as columns along with specification of primary(<<PK>>) and foreign keys (<<FK>>). A UML like investor table is specified in Fig. 5.3.

```
public class Portfolio {
@Id
String portfolioId;
String ownerId; // foreign key

. . .
}
```

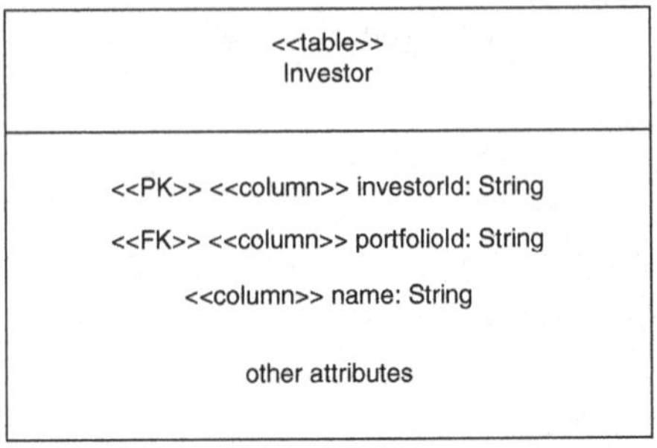

Fig. 5.3 Investor table

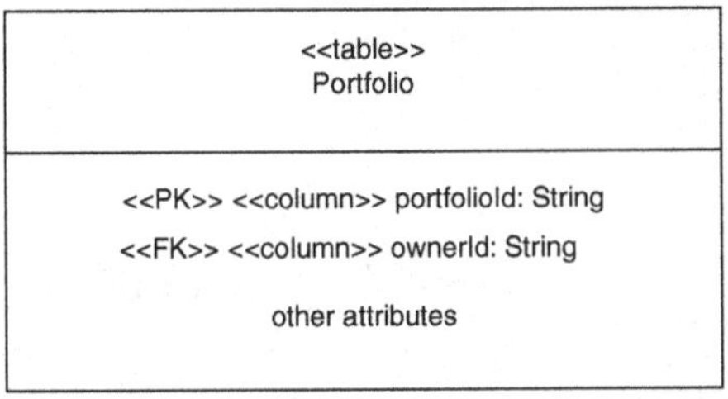

```
                          <<table>>
                          Investor

        <<PK>> <<column>> investorId: String
        <<FK>> <<column>> portfolioId: String
              <<column>> name: String

                    other attributes
```

Fig. 5.4 Portfolio table

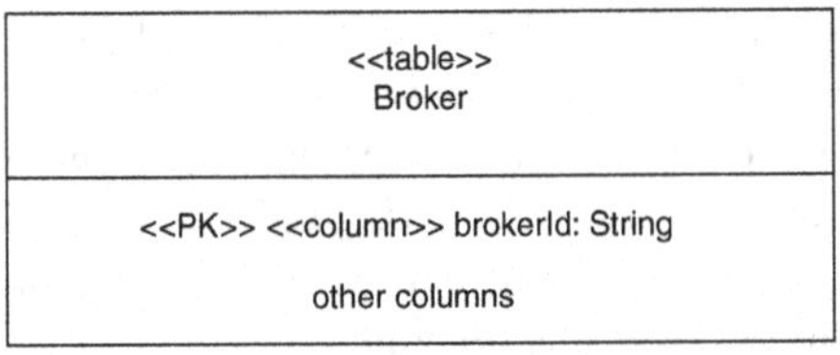

```
                          <<table>>
                          Portfolio

        <<PK>> <<column>> portfolioId: String
        <<FK>> <<column>> ownerId: String

                    other attributes
```

Fig. 5.5 Broker table

```
                          <<table>>
                          Broker

        <<PK>> <<column>> brokerId: String
                    other columns
```

A UML like diagram representing the portfolio table is given in Fig. 5.4.

The one to many relationship between brokers and portfolios is represented by having a field *brokerId* in the class *Portfolio* referencing the primary key of the broker that manages that portfolio.

public class Broker {
@Id
String brokerId;

. . .
}

A diagram representing the broker table is given in Fig. 5.5.

public class Portfolio {
@Id
String portfolioId;
String ownerId; // foreign key
String brokerId; // foreign key

. . .
}

Fig. 5.6 Portfolio table

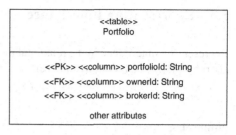

The revised portfolio table is represented in Fig. 5.6.

The many to many relationship between assets and portfolios requires a table that specifies this relationship. Fields of the *PortfolioAsset* class are *portfolioId* and *assetId* referencing primary keys of the classes *Asset* and *Portfolio*.

```
public class Asset {
@Id
String assetId;
. . .
}
```

The table representing the many to many association between portfolios and assets is given in Fig. 5.7.

```
public class PortfolioAsset {
String portfolioId; // foreign key
String assetId; // foreign key

. . .
}
```

Fig. 5.7 PortfolioAsset table

```
                           <<table>>
                          PortfolioAsset

          <<FK>> <<column>> portfolioId: String
          <<FK>> <<column>> assetId: String

                         other columns
```

5.8   Representing Inheritance

Representing inheritance in the relational model comes with nontrivial issues. In the aircraft inheritance hierarchy one technique which is the default in Java Persistence API is to flatten the hierarchy as follows:

public class Aircraft {
@Id
String aircraftId;
String model;
int capacity;
float maxLoad;
String discriminator;
. . .
}

In the corresponding relational representation there is one table given in Fig. 5.8 which contains the attributes of all three entity types in this inheritance hierarchy. In addition, there is a discriminator field which indicates whether a tuple represents a passenger plane of a cargo plane. This discriminator determines the actual subtype of an aircraft object.

Another representation amounts to three different entity types in which the subtypes *PassengerPlane* and *CargoPlane* have all the inherited as well as specific attributes as follows:

public class Aircraft {
@Id
String aircraftId;
String model;
. . .
}

Fig. 5.8 Aircraft table

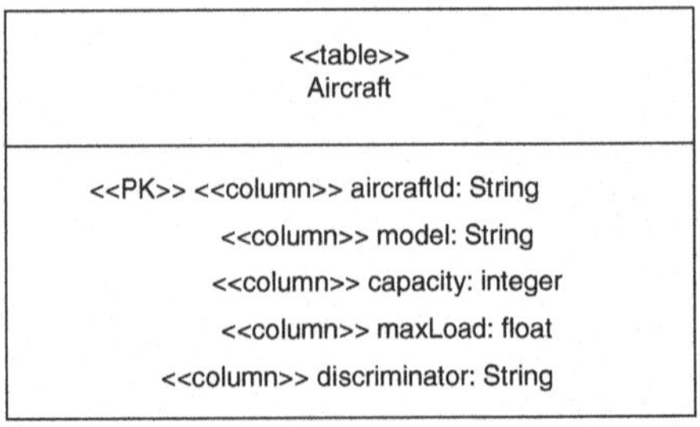

```
                        <<table>>
                         Aircraft

    <<PK>> <<column>> aircraftId: String
           <<column>> model: String
           <<column>> capacity: integer
           <<column>> maxLoad: float
           <<column>> discriminator: String
```

public class PassengerPlane {
@Id
String aircraftId;
String model;
int capacity;

. . .

}

public class CargoPlane {
@Id
String aircraftId;
String model;
float maxLoad;

. . .

}

Finally, in the third representation the table representing the type *Aircraft* has only the generic fields, and the tables representing *PassengerPlane* and *CargoPlane* just the specific attributes in addition to the primary key which identifies the object of type *Aircraft*. The aircraft table in this representation is given in Fig. 5.9.

public class Aircraft {
@Id
String aircraftId;
String model;

. . .

}

The passenger aircraft table corresponding to this representation is given in Fig. 5.10.

Fig. 5.9   Aircraft table

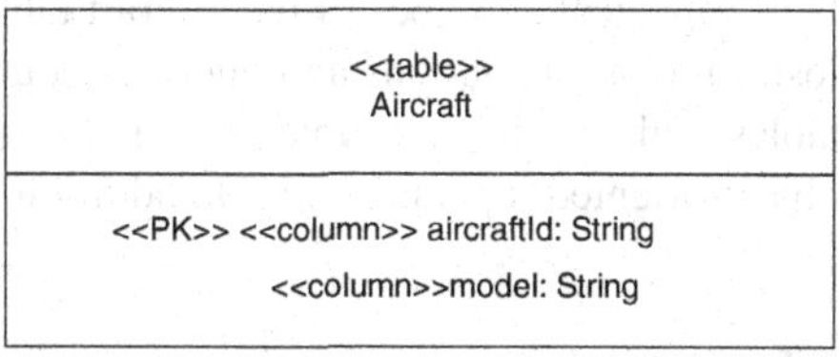

```
                    <<table>>
                    Aircraft

<<PK>> <<column>> aircraftId: String
       <<column>>model: String
```

Fig. 5.10   Passenger plane
table

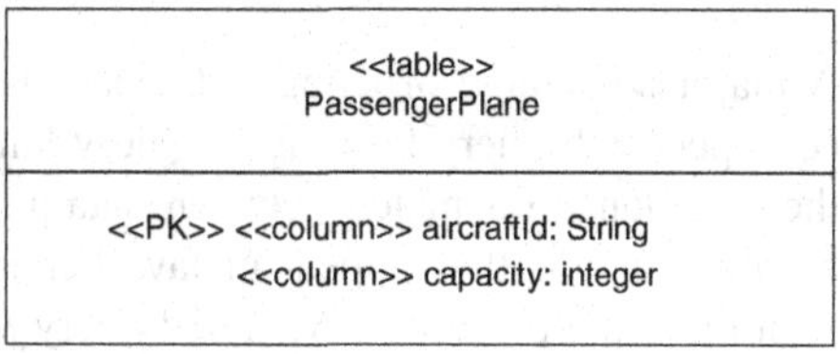

```
                    <<table>>
                    PassengerPlane

<<PK>> <<column>> aircraftId: String
       <<column>> capacity: integer
```

public class PassengerPlane {
@Id
String aircraftId;
int capacity;

. . .

}

The cargo plane table in this representation is given in Fig. 5.11.

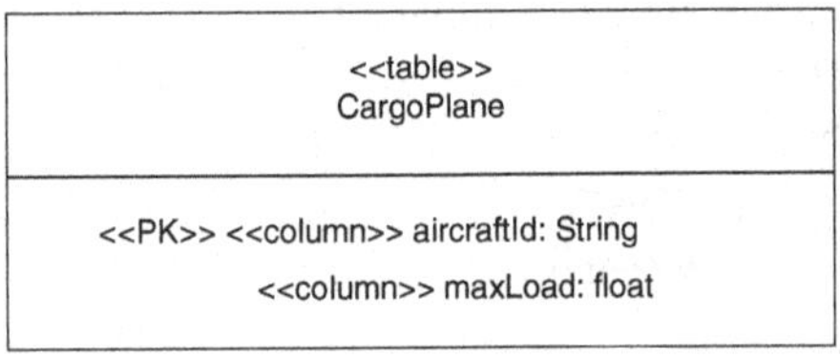

Fig. 5.11   Cargo plane table

```
┌──────────────────────────────────────────────────┐
│                   <<table>>                        │
│                   CargoPlane                       │
├──────────────────────────────────────────────────┤
│     <<PK>> <<column>> aircraftId: String           │
│           <<column>> maxLoad: float                │
└──────────────────────────────────────────────────┘
```

public class CargoPlane {
@Id
String aircraftId;
float maxLoad;

. . .

}

There are different tradeoffs in the above representations none of which is an accurate representation of the object-oriented view of this hierarchy. The single table representation has attributes (columns) that should have undefined values for attributes of cargo planes if a tuple (object) represents a passenger plane. Likewise, a tuple representing a cargo plane should have undefined values of attributes of passenger planes. In the last representation this problem does not occur, but this representation does not indicate that the passenger plane table and the cargo plane table represent subtypes of the aircraft table. That is, the inheritance relationship is lost. In addition, actions and queries about these two subtypes require join of their tables with the aircraft table. This is a complexity which is not required in a true object-oriented representation. In addition, it carries a run-time efficiency penalty.

5.9   Queries

A major advantage of using a database technology is that those technologies are equipped with query languages. Query languages reveal the problem that is called the impedance mismatch between data and programming languages. Queries will be illustrated as they appear in Java Persistence API although JDO also has them with the same problems. A named query *findCheapStocks* is declared representing an SQL query below. The query itself is specified as a string because Java compiler would not know anything about SQL queries. Because of this the query cannot be parsed or type checked at compile time.

```
@NamedQuery(
  name= "findCheapStocks",
  query ="SELECT s FROM Stock
  WHERE s.price < 100"
)
```

A query is executed by invoking the method *createNamedQuery* of the class *EntityManager*. At that point the query is parsed, type checked and executed.

```
@PersistentContext
EntityManager em;
List cheapStocks = em.createNamedQuery(
  "findCheapStocks".getResultList());
```

LINQ (Language Integrated Queries) attempts to resolve the impedance mismatch between data and programming languages by incorporating object-oriented view of SQL queries into C#. LINQ is thus an integrated query and object-oriented language that overcomes many problems that other persistence interfaces have.

LINQ operates on linearly ordered collections or sequences of elements. The interfaces *Enumerator* and *Enumerable* specify the required features that classes specifying enumerable collections must implement. An enumerator object is a cursor over an enumerable collection. It is equipped with a method *moveNext* that moves the cursor to the next element in the underlying sequence. The method *current* returns the current element determined by the cursor.

The two enumerator interfaces are:

```
System.Collections.IEnumerator
System.Collections.Generic.IEnumerator<T>
```

An enumerator class will typically have the following specification:

```
class EnumeratorClass
// implements IEnumerator or IEnumerator<T>
{
  public IteratorVariableType Current { get {...} }
  public bool moveNext() {...}
}
```

The two enumerable interfaces are:

```
System.Collections.IEnumerable
System.Collections.Generic.IEnumerable<T>
```

An enumerable collection will typically have the following specification:

```
class EnumerableClass
 // implements IEnumerable or IEnumerable<T>
{
 public Enumerator getEnumerator() {...}
}
```

A query operates on an enumerable collection transforming it into another sequence representing the result of the query. LINQ queries have the form that is very similar to the SQL *select-from-where* block as illustrated below. The class *Stock* with two properties *StockId* and *Price* is defined as follows. Note that in C# default access right is private, so we did not explicitly specify that in the examples that follow:

```
class Stock {
 String stockId;
 float price;
 // other fields
 // constructor
 public String StockId
 {    get { return stockId; }
 public float Price
 {    get { return price; }
     set { price = value; }
 }
 // other properties
}
```

```
IEnumerable<String> query =
 from s in stocks
 where s.Price < 100
 orderby s.Price
 select s.StockId;
```

The above is just a specification of a query. A query is executed by a *foreach* statement over a query as follows:

```
foreach (String s in query) Console.WriteLine (s);
```

The above SQL-like queries are called comprehension queries. LINQ also has static methods of the class *Enumerable* that perform operations specified in the select, where and order by clauses in comprehension queries. These queries are called lambda queries because arguments are lambda expressions. Specifically, the *where* operator has a predicate specified as a function with the boolean result. The operator *select* projects elements of the input sequence into elements of the output sequence where this projection is specified as a function in lambda notation. Lambda expressions are here simply unnamed (anonymous) functions. The argument is bound to an element of the input sequence, and the result of the function is specified by an expression that shows how the argument is used to compute the result. The previous query has the following lambda query form.

```
IEnumerable<String> query = stocks
  .Where (s ⇒ s.Price < 100)
  .OrderBy (s ⇒ s.Price)
  .Select (s ⇒ s.StockId);
```

Queries can generate enumerable collections of objects rather than just enumerations of values. In the example below the type of objects in the sequence generated by a query is defined first, and then objects of that sequence are generated in the query.

```
class StockPrice {
String stockId;
float price;
 public String StockId;
{get}
 public float Price;
{ get and set }
 // . . .
}

IEnumerable<StockPrice> =
 from s in stocks
 select new StockPrice
     { StockId = s.StockId;
       Price= s.Price;
     }
 where s.Price < 100;
```

Queries can be nested. The query that follows produces a sequence of stock ids of those stocks whose price is larger than the price of any stock of the same company.

```
IEnumerable<String> =
 from s in stocks
 where s.Price() ≥
       Max(from f in stocks
       where s.Company=f.Coompany
       select f.Price)
 select s.StockId;
```

Interfacing with a relational database works as follows. Consider a simple specification of an SQL table *Stock*:

```
create table Stock
(
  StockId varchar(4) not null primary key,
  Price float
)
```

LINQ makes use of optional predefined attributes that C# has to indicate that a class in fact corresponds to a database relation (table). Likewise, using predefined attributes, fields of a class can be specified as columns of a table.

```
[Table]
public class Stock
{
  [Column(IsPrimaryKey=true)]
  public String stockId;
  [Column]
  public float price;
}
```

Access to a relational database is defined by providing a connection string that identifies the database. The class *DataContext* is equipped with a method *getTable* that delivers a table of the database with elements of a given type. There is only one such table in a relational database. So *Table* is a parametric class that implements the interface *Queryable*. This interface extends the interface *Enumerable*, hence queries that operate on sequences can be specified on objects of type *Queryable* as in the example below. While objects of type *Enumerable* are internal sequences, objects of type *Queryable* are meant to be database sequences that allow queries to be optimized.

```
DataContext dataContext = new DataContext ("connection string");
Table<Stock> stocks = dataContext.getTable <Stock>();
IQueryable<String> query =
  from s in stocks
  where s.StockId="SP500"
  orderby s.StockId
  select s.StockId;
```

The above query is executed by the following **foreach** statement:

```
foreach (String s in query) Console.WriteLine(s);
```

5.10   Exercises

1. Specify in the JDO style *BuyAsset* and *SellAsset* transactions of the Investment management application.
2. Specify in the Java persistence API style transactions *BuyAsset* and *SellAsset* for the object-relational model of the Investment management application.
3. Specify a LINQ style interface for the object-relational model of the Investment management application in which classes are specified and annotated as tables.
4. For the object-relational model of the investment management application specify a LINQ query that produces a sequence of all assets (stocks and bonds) in a portfolio of a particular investor.
5. Modify the query from the previous exercise so that it will produce a sequence of pairs of assets of a particular investor along with the value of each asset.
6. Assuming that the queries produced in the previous two exercises are comprehension queries, specify their corresponding lambda queries.
7. Specify a LINQ style interface for the Flight management model in which classes are specified and annotated as tables.
8. Specify in the Java Persistence API style transactions *ScheduleFlight* and *CancelFlight* of the object-relational model of this application.
9. Specify in the JDO style transactions *ScheduleCourse* and *DeleteCourse* for the object-oriented Course management model.
10. Specify in the JDO style transactions *EnrollInCourse* and *DropCourse* for the object-oriented Course management model.
11. Specify an object-relational model of the Course management application as in Java Persistence API.
12. Specify in the Java Persistence API style transactions *EnrollInCourse* and *DropCourse* for the object-relational model of the Course management application.

Chapter 6
Software Verification

Promoting assertion languages comes with several challenges. OCL is a specification language independent of any particular object-oriented programming language. A major technical challenge is integrating such declarative specifications into a full-fledged object-oriented programming language in such a way that those specifications are enforced in the procedural code. This would be preferably done statically, i.e., by inspecting the code equipped with assertions and verifying that the code satisfies the specifications. If that is not possible, then a dynamic verification should be in place, i.e., the specifications will be enforced as the code is executed. Extending an object-oriented programming language with declarative specifications such as those in OCL requires significant changes of the underlying object-oriented programming language and a complex implementation technique if static verification of assertions is supported.

In this chapter a system called Code Contracts is used to specify assertions with no changes to the underlying C# language. Code Contracts is at the moment an open source system developed at Microsoft Research. All assertions of Code Contracts appear as invocations of methods of the class *Contract*. The actual assertions are specified as boolean expressions, arguments of these methods. This approach leads to dynamic checking of assertions as methods of the class *Contract* are executed. Code Contracts also has some static checking capabilities.

6.1 Preconditions and Postconditions

In this section we will show how pre and post conditions of methods are specified in Code Contracts.

© Springer International Publishing AG 2017   139
S. Alagić, *Software Engineering: Specification, Implementation, Verification*,
DOI 10.1007/978-3-319-61518-9_6

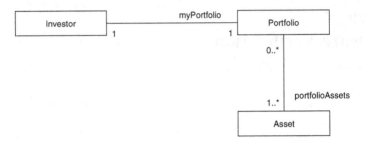

Fig. 6.1 Associations for investing

6.1.1 Investment Management Application

The two critical methods in the investment management application that correspond to two use cases are buying and selling assets. The associations relevant to buying and selling assets are given in Fig. 6.1.

The precondition of the method *buyAsset* requires that the investor's portfolio does not already contain that asset. The postcondition ensures that the asset is in the investor's portfolio

```
void buyAsset(Asset a)
{ Contract.Requires(!this.getMyPortfolio().getPortfolioAssets().Contains(a));
  Contract.Ensures(this.getMyPortfolio().getPortfolioAssets().Contains(a));
// code
}
```

The precondition of the method *sellAsset* requires that the asset is in the investor's portfolio. The postcondition ensures that the asset is not any more in the investor's portfolio.

```
void sellAsset(Asset a)
{ Contract.Requires(this.getMyPortfolio().getPortfolioAssets().Contains(a));
  Contract.Ensures(!this.getMyPortfolio().getPortfolioAssets().Contains(a));
// code
}
```

Pure methods, i.e., methods with no side effects, of the class *Investor* used in the above specifications are annotated as follows:

```
class Investor: InvestorI {
[Pure]
Portfolio getMyPortfolio()
{// code
  }
```

```
void buyAsset(Asset a)
{ // code
 }
void sellAsset(Asset a)
{ // code
 }
}
```

The class *Portfolio* has the following structure in which pure methods are annotated as such.

```
class Portfolio: IPortfolio {
[Pure]
Collection<Asset> getPortfolioAssets()
{ // code
 }
[Pure]
Broker getBroker()
{ // code
 }
[Pure]
Investor getInvestor()
{// code
 }
}
```

6.1.2   Course Management Application

Consider the class *Registrar* that implements the interface *IRegistrar* of the course management application. The relevant associations are given in Fig. 6.2.

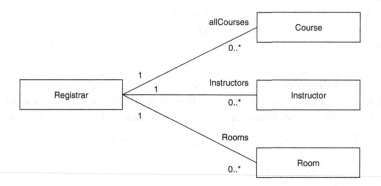

Fig. 6.2   Associations for scheduling a course

Specification of the method *scheduleCourse* includes two preconditions expressed by invoking the method *Requires* of the class *Contract*. The first precondition

Contract.Requires(!this.getAllCourses().Contains(c))

requires that the course to be scheduled is not already scheduled, i.e., that it is not in the list of scheduled courses. The second precondition

Contract.Requires(Contract.Exists(this.getRooms(), r => r.suitableFor(c))

requires that there is a suitable room for scheduling the course. The postcondition

Contract.Ensures(this.getAllCourses().Contains(c))

expressed invoking the method *Ensures* of the class *Contract* ensures that the course is actually scheduled, i.e. it exists in the collection of all scheduled courses.

Assertions are specified as expressions of the boolean type that appear as arguments of the methods of the class *Contract*. Boolean expressions of object-oriented programming languages do not include universal and existential quantifications over collection types. Code Contracts solves this problem by having method *ForAll* and *Exists* of the class *Contract*. These methods take two parameters. The first parameter (this.getRooms() in the above assertion) specifies the collection over which quantification occurs. The second parameter

r => r.suitableFor(c)

in the above assertion is a C# lambda expression. This expression specifies a variable that ranges over that collection and a boolean expression that elements that qualify must satisfy. In the case of the *ForAll* method, all elements of the collection must satisfy that condition in order for the assertion to be true. In the case of the method *Exists* at least one element must satisfy the condition for the assertion to be true.

```
void scheduleCourse(Course c)
{ Contract.Requires(!this.getAllCourses().Contains(c));
   Contract.Requires(Contract.Exists(
      this.getRooms(), r => r.suitableFor(c))
 Contract.Ensures(this.getAllCourses().Contains(c));
// code
}
```

The precondition of the method *deleteCourse* requires that the course to be deleted is actually in the list of all scheduled courses. The postcondition ensures that the course is actually deleted from the collection of all scheduled courses.

```
void deleteCourse(Course c)
{ Contract.Requires(this.getAllCourses().Contains(c));
  Contract.Ensures(!this.getAllCourses().Contains(c));
// code
}
```

Boolean expressions that appear as arguments of the methods such as *Requires*, *Ensures*, *ForAll*, *Exists* and other methods of the class *Contract* include invocations of other methods. The above example contains invocation of the methods *getAll-Courses*, and *getAllRooms*. These methods must be pure functions which means that they cause no side effects. Pure methods are annotated by the attribute [Pure]. So the structure of the class *Registrar* looks like this.

```
class Registrar: IRegistrar {
[Pure]
Collection<Course> getAllCourses()
{ // code
 }
[Pure]
Collection<Instructor> getInstructors()
{// code
 }
[Pure]
Collection<Students> getStudents()
{ // code
 }
[Pure]
Collection<Room> getRooms()
{ // code
 }
void scheduleCourse(Course c)
{ // code
 }
void deleteCourse(Course c)
{ // code
 }
}
```

The associations relevant for enrolling in a course are specified in Fig. 6.3. The first precondition of the method *enrollInCourse* of the class *Student*

```
Contract.Requires(!this.getMyCourses().Contains(c))
```

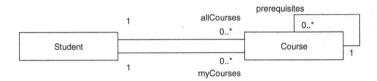

Fig. 6.3   Associations for enrolling in a course

requires that the course is not already in the collection of all courses of the receiver student object. The second precondition

Contract.Requires(Contract.ForAll(c.getPrerequisites(),
   p => this.getMyCourses().Contains(p)))

specifies that the student satisfies the prerequisites for the course. This precondition involves quantification over all prerequisites of the course and checking whether those prerequisite courses are in the set of courses already taken by the student. This quantification is expressed by invoking the method *ForAll* of the class *Contract* as explained above. The postcondition

Contract.Ensures(this.getMyCourses().Contains(c))

ensures that the course is in the collection of all courses of the student.


```
void enrollInCourse(Course c)
{ Contract.Requires(!this.getMyCourses().Contains(c));
  Contract.Requires(Contract.ForAll(
      c.getPrerequisites(), p => this.getMyCourses().Contains(p)));
  Contract.Ensures(this.getMyCourses().Contains(c));
// code
}
```

The precondition of the method *dropCourse*

Contract.Requires(this.getMyCourses().Contains(c))

requires that the course is in the collection of courses taken by the student. The postcondition

Contract.Ensures(!this.getMyCourses().Contains(c))

ensures that the course is not in that collection any more.


```
void dropCourse(Course c)
{ Contract.Requires(this.getMyCourses().Contains(c));
  Contract.Ensures(!this.getMyCourses().Contains(c));
// code
}
```

The above specifications contain invocations of the pure method *getMyCourses*. A reference to the state before method execution is accomplished by a parametric method *OldValue< T >*. For example, an additional postcondition of the method *enrollInCourse* might be:

Contract.Ensures(this.getMyCourses().Count()=
OldValue<int>(this.getMyCourses().Count()) +1

A reference to the result of a method is accomplished by invoking a parametric method *Result< T >* of the class *Contract*. For example, the postcondition of the method

float gradeAverage()

of the class *Student* may be defined as follows:

Contract.Ensures(Result<float> >= 1 &&
     Result<float> <= 5)

The structure of the class *Student* in which pure methods are annotated with the attribute [Pure] looks like this:

```
class Student: IStudent {
[Pure]
Collection<Course> getAllCourses()
{ // code
 }
[Pure]
Collection<Course> getMyCourses();
{// code
 }
void enrollInCourse(Course c)
{ // code
 }
void dropCourse(Course c)
{ // code
 }
}
```

6.2   Object Invariants

The class *Flight* shows how Code Contracts specifies object invariants. An object invariant is specified in a distinguished method marked with a special attribute [ContractInvariantMethod]. This method contains calls of the method *Invariant* of the class *Contract*. Code Contract enforces object invariants after execution of public methods.

Object invariants of the class *Flight* are specified below in the method *Object-Invariant*. Each invariant is specified by invoking the method *Invariant* of the class *Contract*. The first invariant requires that the origin and the destination of a flight must be different. The second invariant specifies that the departure time must precede the arrival time. The third invariant specifies that if the flight status is idle, then the current time precedes the departure time. The third invariant specifies that if the current time is past the departure time and it precedes the arrival time, the flight status must be either takeoff, flying or landing. The form of the Boolean expression in the third invariant is a consequence of the lack of the explicit Boolean operation of implication in C#. This pattern will appear in other assertions in this chapter.

```
class Flight: IFlight {
  // fields etc.
[ContractInvariantMethod]
void ObjectInvariant()
{ Contract.Invariant(
      this.to ! = this.from);
  Contract.Invariant(
      this.departureTime.precedes(this.arrivalTime));
  Contract.Invariant(
      this.flightStatus ! = "idle" || Time.now().precedes(this.departureTime));
  Contract.Invariant(
      Time.now().after(this.departureTime) &&
      (!Time.now().precedes(arrivalTime) ||
      (flightStatus = "takeoff" || flightStatus = "flying" ||
      this.flightStatus = "landing")))
// dummy code
  }
}
```

Note that the method *ObjectInvariant* has a body which contains some dummy code just to satisfy the C# compiler. This is a consequence of the design decision that the assertions must be added to C# without any changes to the language so that the C# compiler will compile the code with assertions.

The first object invariant of the class *FlightSchedule* specifies that the *flightId* attribute is a key in the collection of all flights. That is, if two flights have the same value of the *flightId* attribute, then they are in fact the same flight. Note the usage of the *ForAll* method of the class *Contract*. The key constraint requires universal quantification and two range variables in the lambda expression. The second invariant specifies a referential integrity constraint which requires that a flight refers to an existing plane. The third and the fourth invariants specify that a flight must refer to existing airports as its origin and its destination. Note that these constraints require first the *ForAll* method because the assertion applies to all flights.

The nested usage of the method *Exists* then guarantees that the flight origin and its destination refer to an existing airport. This involves existential quantification over all airports.

```
class FlightSchedule: IFlightSchedule {
  //... ;
[ContractInvariantMethod]
void ObjectInvariant()
{ Contract.Invariant(
  Contract.ForAll( this.flights,
      (f1,f2) =>!(f1.flightId = f2.flightId) || f1.Equals(f2))
  Contract.Invariant(ForAll(this.flights,
      f =>Contract.Exists(this.planes,
      p => f.plane=p))
  Contract.Invariant(Contract.ForAll(this.flights,
      f => Contract.Exists(this.airports,
      a => f.from=a)));
  Contract.Invariant(Contract.ForAll(this.flights,
      f => Contract.Exists(this.airports,
      a => f.to=a)));
// dummy code
  }
}
```

The associations relevant for flight scheduling are given in Fig. 6.4.

The first precondition of the method *scheduleFlight* requires that the origin and the destination airport of the flight to be scheduled must be different. The second precondition requires that the departure time must precede the arrival time. The third precondition requires that the flight with the *flightId* given as the first argument of this method does not already exist in the schedule. The fourth precondition requires that the plane given as an argument of this method actually exists. The postcondition ensures that a flight with a given flight id actually exists in the flight schedule.

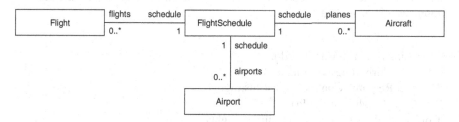

Fig. 6.4   Associations for flight scheduling

```
void scheduleFlight(String flightId,
             Airport from,to,
             Time departureTime, arrivalTime
             Aircraft plane)
{ Contract.Requires(!to.Equals(from));
  Contract.Requires(departureTime.precedes(arrivalTime));
  Contract.Requires(Contract.ForAll(this.flights,
      f => f.flightId ! = flightId);
  Contract.Requires(ContractExists(this.planes,
      p => plane=p))
  Contract.Ensures(Contract.Exists(this.flights,
      f => f.flightId=flightId))
// code
}
```

The first precondition of the method *cancelFlight* requires that a flight with a flight id given as the argument of this method actually exists in the schedule. The second precondition requires that the status of the flight to be cancelled is not landing. The postcondition ensures that the cancelled flight is not in the flight schedule any more.

```
void cancelFlight(String flightId)
  Contract.Requires(ContractExists(this.flights,
      f => f.flightId=flightId))
  Contract.Requires(ContractForAll(this.flights,
      f => f.flightId ! = flightId || f.flightStatus ! = "landing"))
  Contract.Ensures(Contract.ForAll(this.flights,
      f => f.flightId ! = flightId))
// code
}
```

The first precondition of the method *redirectFlight* requires that the flight to be redirected exists in the schedule of all flights. The second precondition requires that the new destination is different from the flight's origin. The postcondition ensures that the redirected flight indeed has a new destination as specified by the second argument of this method.

```
void redirectFlight(String flightId,
           Airport newDestination)
  Contract.Requires(ContractExists(this.flights,
      f => f.flightId=flightId))
  Contract.Requires(ContractForAll(this.flights,
      f => f.flightId ! = flightId || f.from ! = newDestination))
  Contract.Ensures(Contract.ForAll(this.flights,
```

```
        f => f.flightId ! = flightId ||
        f.destination.Equals(newDestination)))
// code
}
```

6.3 Assertions and Inheritance

The interplay of assertions and inheritance leads to nontrivial subtleties that we discussed in Chap. 2. The reason is that behavior of an object is determined by the assertions specified in its class. Consider now a subclass equipped with assertions that determine behavior of objects of that subclass. Since an object of a subclass may be substituted where an object of the superclass is expected, one would naturally expect that the substituted object behaves like an object of the superclass. This reasoning leads to rules that apply to assertions in a subclass with respect to the assertions in its superclass.

These rules will be explained looking again at a class *Airport* and its subclass *InternationalAirport*, both equipped with assertions that will be now expressed in Code Contracts. The invariant of the class Airport requires that an airport has at least one runway and at most 30 as in Fig. 6.5

```
class Airport {
    ... ;
[ContractInvariantMethod]
void ObjectInvariant ()
{ Contract.Invariant(this.numOfRunways >= 1 &&
        this.numOfRunways <= 30)
// dummycode
}
```

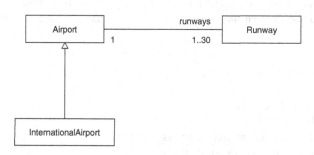

Fig. 6.5 Inheritance for airports

The precondition of the method *addRunway* of the class *Airport* requires that a runway to be added is not already one of the airport's runways. The postcondition guarantees that the new runway is indeed one of the airport's runways.

```
void addRunway(Runway strip)
{ Contract.Requires(Contract.ForAll(this.runways,
      r => !r.Equals(strip)));
  Contract.Ensures(Contract.Exists(this.runways,
      r => r.Equals(strip)))
// code
}
```

The first precondition of the method *closeRunway* requires that the runway to be closed is indeed one of the existing runways. The second precondition requires that the number of runways of the airport is greater than 1, or else closing the only runway will violate the invariant. The postcondition ensures that the closed runway is not any more one of the airport's runways.

```
void closeRunway(Runway strip)
{ Contract.Requires(Contract.Exists(this.runways,
      r => r.Equals(strip)));
  Contract.Requires(this.numOfRunways > 1);
  Contract.Ensures(Contract.ForAll(this.runways,
      r => !r.Equals(strip)));
// code
}
```

Consider now the class *InternationalAirport* derived by inheritance from the class *Airport*. The object invariant of the class *Airport* is inherited in the class *InternationalAirport* or else an object of a class *InternationalAirport* would not behave like an object of the class *Airport*. In addition, the object invariant of the class *InternationalAirport* is strengthened by adding two new invariants. The first invariant requires that an international airport has at least 10 runways. The second invariant requires that an international airport must have at least one international runway.

```
class InternationaAirport: Airport {
   ... ;
[ContractInvariantMethod]
void ObjectInvariant ()
{ Contract.Invariant(this.numOfRunways >= 10);
  Contract.Invariant(Contract.Exists(this.runways,
      r => r.international=true))
// dummy code
}
```

The method *addRunway* is inherited as defined in the class *Airport*. In the method *closeRunway* of the class *InternationalAirport* we would like to strengthen the inherited precondition by requiring that the runway to be closed is not the only international runway. But strengthening the preconditions of an inherited method violates the behavioral compatibility rules so that an international airport object would not behave like an airport object.

Strengthening the postcondition of an inherited method does not create such a problem. The first postcondition ensures that the number of runways is greater than or equal to 10. The second postcondition ensures that the airport contains at least one international runway.

```
void closeRunway(Runway strip)
{ Contract.Ensures(this.noOfRunways >= 10);
  Contract.Ensures(Contract.Exist(this.runways,
  r => r.international=true))
// code
}
```

6.4   Assertions for Interfaces

Interfaces in Java and C# suffer from a major contradiction. The only way to understand the specific meaning of the methods of an interface is to look into the method code in the implementing class, contrary to the intent for introducing interfaces. This is why specifying assertions in interfaces is so very important. However, assertions such as object invariants often require the knowledge of the object state which is not available in interfaces. Code Contracts resolves this situation by specifying assertions of an interface in a special class associated with the interface. This class is used only to specify the assertions and it is never executed like other classes. But these assertions will be enforced in any class that implements the interface.

Consider an interface *IRegistrar* as specified below.

```
[ContractClass(typeof(ContractforIRegistrar))]
interface IRegistrar
{ void scheduleCourse(Course c);
  void deleteCourse(Course c);
}
```

The assertions for this interface are specified in the associated class *Contract-forIRegistrar*. Special attributes of the interface and the associated class specify this relationship. In the class *ContractforIRegistrar* the preconditions and the postconditions of the methods *scheduleCourse* and *deleteCourse* are specified as previously shown. Dummy bodies of these methods will never be executed and are required only to satisfy the C# compiler.

```
[ContractClassFor(typeof(IRegistrar))]
sealed class ContractforIRegistrar: IRegistrar
{ void scheduleCourse(Course c)
{ Contract.Requires(!this.getAllCourses().Contains(c));
  Contract.Requires(Contract.Exists(
      this.getAllRooms(), r => r.suitableFor(c))
  Contract.Ensures(this.getAllCourses().Contains(c));
// dummy code
}
void deleteCourse(Course c)
{ Contract.Requires(this.getAllCourses().Contains(c));
  Contract.Ensures(!this.getAllCourses().Contains(c));
// dummy code
  }
}
```

The above described situation is presented in a UML like diagram in Fig. 6.6.

The contracts for the interface *IStudent* are specified in the class *ContractforIStudent*.

```
[ContractClass(typeof(ContractforIStudent))]
interface IStudent
{ void enrollInCourse(Course c);
  void dropCourse(Course c);
}
```

The methods *enrollInCourse* and *dropCourse* are equipped with preconditions and postconditions as previously specified.

```
[ContractClassFor(typeof(IStudent))]
sealed class ContractforIStudent: IStudent
void enrollInCourse(Course c)
{ Contract.Requires(!this.getMyCourses().Contains(c));
```

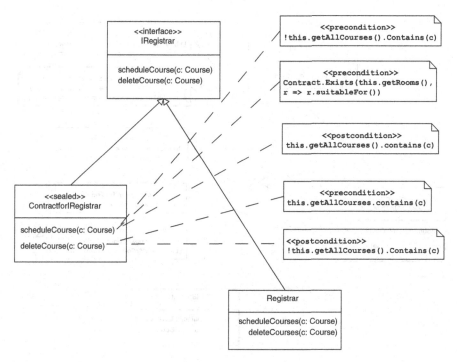

Fig. 6.6   Constraints for the interface IRegistrar

ContractRequires(Contract.ForAll(
        c.getPrerequisites(), p => this.getMyCourses().Contains(p)));
    Contract.Ensures(this.getMyCourses().Contains(c));
// dummy code
    }
void dropCourse(Course c)
{ Contract.Requires(this.getMyCourses().Contains(c));
    Contract.Ensures(!this.getMyCourses().Contains(c));
// dummycode
    }
}

The above described technique for specifying assertions for the interface *IStudent* is presented in a UML like diagram in Fig. 6.7.

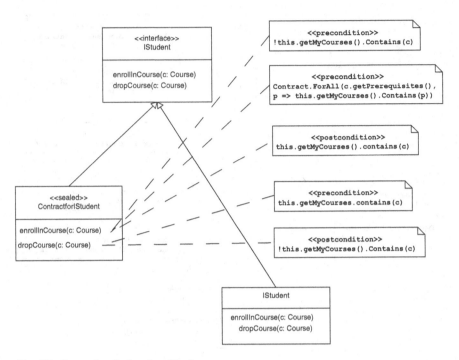

Fig. 6.7   Constraints for interface IStudent

6.5   Sample Application

The tournament management application has several types of users, two of which
we specify. A tournament has a manager and a list of players. This is represented in
Fig. 6.8. The notation in this figure indicates that a tournament has a unique manager
and it is associated with multiple players.

The class *Tournament* given below specifies the features of tournament objects. It
contains self-explanatory fields, properties and a constructor. Note that in C# default
access right is private, so the fields *name* and *manager* are private.

```
class Tournament {
  String name;
  Manager manager;
  List<Player> players = new List<Player>();
  // other fields
  // constructor
  public String Name
  {    get { return name; }
       set { name = value; }
```

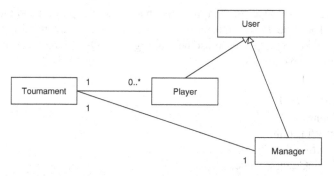

Fig. 6.8 Tournament management application

```
}
// other properties
}
```

Generic properties of a tournament user are specified below in a class *User* in the C# style. As explained in Chap. 3, a property in C# is a pair of methods. The method *get* returns the value of a property and the method *set* assigns a value to a property. Note that **private** is the default accessibility for members of a class in C#. So in the above example the underlying (backing) fields are private and the properties are public.

In the class *User* the invariants are that the user name cannot be null and the user ID number cannot be null.

```
abstract class User {
  String IDNum;
  String name;
  String role;
  [ContractInvariantMethod]
  void ObjectInvariant() {
      Contract.Invariant(this.UserName != null);
      Contract.Invariant(this.ID != null);
  }
public String ID
  {   get { return IDNum; }
      set { IDNum = value; }
  }
  public String UserName
  {   get { return name; }
      set { user = value; }
  }
  // Role property
}
```

There are two subtypes of the type *User* that we define: players and tournament managers. The type *Player* introduces an additional invariant requiring that the number of wins of a player must be nonnegative. Other object invariants are inherited from the class *User*.

```
class Player : User {
 int winCount;
 public int WinCount
 {     get { return winCount; }
      set { winCount = value; }
 }
 //other properties
 [ContractInvariantMethod]
 void ObjectInvariant() {
      Contract.Invariant(this.WinCount >= 0);
 }
 // constructor and other methods
}
```

The class *Manager* strengthens the object invariant. In addition to the invariants inherited from the class *User*, the class *Manager* requires that the role of a tournament manager contains the word "MANAGER".

```
class Manager : User {
 // fields
 [ContractInvariantMethod]
 void ObjectInvariant() {
 { Contract.Invariant(Role.ToUpper().Contains("MANAGER"));
 }
// methods
}
```

Consider now a method for adding a new player to a tournament. This would be a method of the overall application class *TournamentManagement* that we do not show. The method *addPlayer* requires a pure method *playerRegistered* that checks whether the player to be added is already in the list of players of the given tournament.

```
[Pure]
public boolean playerRegistered(Player newPlayer, Tournament tournament) {
 foreach (Player player in tournament.players)
 { if (newPlayer.UserName.ToUpper().Equals(player.UserName.ToUpper()))
      return true;
 }
 return false;
}
```

The preconditions of the method *addPlayer* require that the given player and the tournament must be non null.

Contract.Requires(newPlayer != **null**);
Contract.Requires(tournament != **null**);

In addition, the third precondition requires that the player does not already participate in the tournament.

Contract.Requires(!playerRegistered(newPlayer, tournament));

The postconditions are that the player participates in the tournament (i.e., it has been added to the list of players).

Contract.Ensures(playerRegistered(newPlayer, tournament));

In addition, the postconditions require that the number of players has been increased by one.

Contract.Ensures((tournament.Players.Count) =
    (Contract.OldValue(tournament.Players.Count) + 1));

A reference to the number of players before the method execution is specified by invocation of the method *OldValue* of the class *Contract*. *Players* is a property whose underlying field is *players*.


```
public void addPlayer(Player newPlayer, Tournament tournament) {
Contract.Requires(newPlayer != null);
Contract.Requires(tournament != null);
Contract.Requires(! playerRegistered(newPlayer, tournament));
Contract.Ensures(playerRegistered(newPlayer, tournament));
Contract.Ensures((tournament.Players.Count) =
  (Contract.OldValue(tournament.Players.Count) + 1));
tournament.Players.Add(newPlayer);
}
```

Specification of assertions that require universal and existential quantification is accomplished by using methods *ForAll* and *Exists* of the class *Contracts*.

Universal quantification is used in order to specify an assertion that the list of players contains no null entries.

Contract.Invariant(Contract.ForAll(Players, p **implies** p != **null**));

Existential quantification is used to specify an assertion that the list of players contains at least one player whose total number of wins is greater than zero.

Contract.Invariant(Contract.Exists(Players, p **implies** p.WinCount > 0));

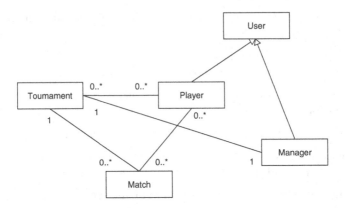

Fig. 6.9 Tournaments with matches

The simplified view of the tournament management application can be general-
ized so that a tournament has a collection of matches. A match has a number of
players, and a player participates in a number of matches. This extended view is
presented in Fig. 6.9. The associated constraints are elaborated in the exercises.

6.6 Transaction Verification

In Chap. 5 we presented a view in which use cases are typically implemented
as transactions. In addition, we discussed software technologies for managing
persistent data which most software projects require. In this and the following
section we discuss more advanced software verification techniques that apply to
verification of transactions.

The current object technology has nontrivial problems in specifying just the
classical database integrity constraints, such as keys and referential integrity.
No industrial database technology allows object-oriented schemas equipped with
general integrity constraints. More general constraints that are not necessarily
classical database constraints come from complex application environments and
they are often critical for correct functioning of those applications.

Since the integrity constraints cannot be specified in a declarative fashion,
the only option is to enforce them procedurally with nontrivial implications on
efficiency and reliability. Expensive recovery procedures may be required when
a transaction violates the constraints at run-time. A core idea is that if a static
verification of a transaction does not succeed, such a transaction should never be
executed. Knowing in advance that a transaction will violate the integrity constraints
makes a huge difference in any complex application environment as it statically
eliminates the consequences of running such a transaction against the database.

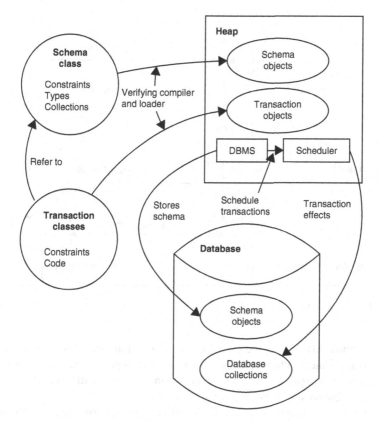

Fig. 6.10 Transaction verification environment

The overall transaction verification environment is represented in Fig. 6.10. A schema is a typed specification of persistent (database) objects that are typically collections. A schema is specified as a class. The novelty is that a schema class will contain possibly quite general database integrity constraints specified as the schema invariant.

A transaction is a parametric class. It is instantiated with a specific schema to which the transaction is bound. Unlike typical database transactions, transactions are in this environment equipped with constraints specifying the transaction precondition and the transaction postcondition. In addition to these constraints, a transaction is required to satisfy the schema invariant.

Both the schema class and the transaction class are compiled by a verifying compiler. This compiler will statically verify that the transaction code satisfies the transaction specification. This means that if the transaction precondition and the schema invariant hold before the transaction is executed, the transaction postcondition and the schema invariant will hold at the point of the transaction commit.

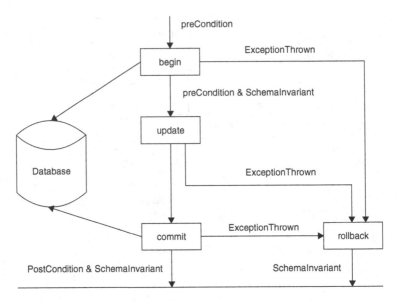

Fig. 6.11   Transaction execution

The schema class object and each specific transaction class object are loaded on the heap. The schema class object is also promoted to persistence, i.e., stored into the database. Managing persistent objects (storing, accessing (querying), updating, deleting) is delegated to a database management system.

Collections of database objects will conform to type and constraint specifications in the persistent schema object. Transaction actions on persistent objects that do not satisfy this requirement will have no impact on the database. Violations will be detected either at compile time by the verifying compiler, or at run time by dynamic checks for some constraints, such as preconditions. This is a major distinction between this environment and a typical database environments.

Transaction execution structure is presented in Fig. 6.11. The transaction first invokes the method *begin*. The precondition of this method is the transaction precondition. The postcondition ensures two things before the actual transaction code is executed. The first one is that the transaction precondition still holds. The second is that the schema integrity constraints hold. The method *update* in Fig. 6.11 actually represents the transaction code. If an exception happens during transaction execution and it is not handled, the method *rollback* is executed. This method erases all effects of the transaction and restores a consistent database state. The postcondition of the *rollback* method is that the database integrity constraints hold i.e., a consistent database state is restored. If no exception occurs the method *commit* is invoked. If it is successful, the postcondition of this method ensures that both the transaction postcondition and the database integrity constraint hold after commit.

We will explain the main issues in transaction verification using the notation of Code Contracts although Code Contracts is not targeted to transaction technology. Specific database schemas are derived from the class *Schema* which is equipped with an abstract boolean method *integrityConstraints*. This method will be overridden in a particular schema to specify the specific integrity constraints.

```
public abstract class Schema {
[Pure]
public static abstract bool integrityConstraints();
}
```

The class *Transaction* is parametric. Its type parameter represents the database schema with respect of which the transaction is defined. This is why the bound for the type parameter is the class *Schema*. Transaction precondition and the postcondition are specified as abstract boolean methods to be overridden in a specific transaction class.

As explained above, the method *begin* requires that the transaction precondition holds before this method is executed. The postcondition of the method *begin* ensures that the transaction postcondition and the database integrity constraints hold before the transaction body is executed. The postcondition of the method *commit* ensures that the transaction postcondition and the database integrity constraints hold after a successful commit. The postcondition of the method *rollback* guarantees that a consistent database state is restored after roll back.

```
public abstract class Transaction<T> where T: Schema {
[Pure]
public abstract bool preCondition();
[Pure]
public abstract bool postCondition();
public sealed begin() {
  Contract.Requires(this.preCondition());
  Contract.Ensures(this.preCondition());
  Contract.Ensures(T.integrityConstraints());
// system implementation
}
public sealed commit() {
  Contract.Ensures(this.postCondition());
  Contract.Ensures(T.integrityConstraints());
// system implementation
}
public sealed rollBack() {
  Contract.Ensures(T.integrityConstraints());
// system implementation
}
}
```

A specific schema *FlightSchedule* is derived from the class *Schema* by inheritance. This class overrides the abstract method *integrityConstraints*. In order to simplify the presentation we specify only one integrity constraint which asserts that *flightId* is a key in the table *flights*.

```
public class FlightSchedule: Schema {
public Table<Flight> flights;
[Pure]
public static abstract bool integrityConstraints() {
return(Contract.ForAll(this.flights,
     (f1,f2) => (f1.flightId != f2.flightId || f1.Equals(f2)));

class Flight {
String flightId;
 . . .
 }
}
```

A specific transaction class *ScheduleFlight* is defined with respect to the schema *FlightSchedule*. The inherited abstract methods *preCondition* and *postCondition* are overridden. The method *preCondition* asserts that the new flight does not exist in the schedule. The method *postCondition* asserts that it does. Now the actual *schedule* method that represents the transaction body is specified with the precondition and the postcondition as defined by the above two methods. The method *schedule* represents the actual transaction update action.

```
public class ScheduleFlight: Transaction<FlightSchedule> {
[Pure]
public bool preCondition() {
  Flight newFlight = get new flight;
  return Contract.ForAll(FlightSchedule.flights,
      f => f.flightId ! = newFlight.flightId)
[Pure]
public bool bool postCondition() {
  Flight newFlight = get new flight;
  return Contract.Exists(FlightSchedule.flights,
      f => f.flightId = newFlight.flightId)
}
public void schedule(Flight newFlight) {
Contract.Requires(this.preCondition());
Contract.Ensures(this.postCondition());
// code
 }
 }
```

A specific transaction requires first of all creation of a transaction object of the appropriate type. The method *begin* is invoked first and then the actual scheduling method. Afterwards an attempt is made to commit the transaction. If an exception occurs the *rollback* method is invoked.

```
Flight newFlight = . . .
ScheduleFlight Tx = new ScheduleFlight();
try {
 Tx.begin();
 Tx.schedule(newFlight);
 Tx.commit();
 }
catch (Exception ex)
 { Tx.rollBack;}
```

6.7   Integrated Specification and Verification Systems

Code Contract was designed with a requirement that constraints are added to C# without any changes to the language. Since constraints appear as invocations of methods of the class *Contract* whose arguments are just Boolean expressions of C#, the C# compiler has no problem in compiling them. Some changes were still required in the compiled code so that the constraints will be handled correctly.

The reality is that constraints are declarative specifications whose expressions are much more general than expressions of object-oriented programming languages. So a more ambitious goal is to extend the underlying programming language to support the expressions required by a constraint language. An extended compiler of the extended language would then be required. One such prototype to be discussed in this section is Spec#, an extension of C#. Spec# has a verifying compiler that statically checks whether the procedural C# code satisfies the constraints. This requires a complex underlying architecture which is one of the reasons why this technology has not been widely used. But it is the future of software verification and we discuss it as such.

In addition to constraints, Spec# has an ownership model which allows specification of complex objects defined by the aggregation abstraction. It restricts updates to components of such complex objects requiring that those updates must first access the owner before mutating the components. In a constraint-oriented ownership model these updates are required to comply with the integrity constraints that apply to entire complex objects.

Fig. 6.12 Associations for
the stock market application

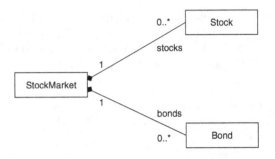

Consider a complex object of type *StockMarket.* Components of a complex object
of this type are a collection of stocks and a collection of bonds, as in Fig. 6.12.
A stock market object owns its component objects. In Spec# this is specified as
follows:

class StockMarket: Schema {
[SpecPublic][Rep] **private** Set<Stock> stocks;
[SpecPublic][Rep] **private** Set<Broker> brokers;

// . . .

}

The attribute [Rep] indicates that stocks and bonds are components of the stock
market object. The attribute [SpecPublic] indicates that the set of stocks and the
set of bonds are exposed as public only for specification purposes. This makes it
possible to specify object invariants of this schema which are publicly available.

The integrity constraints of a schema are specified in its invariant. The schema
StockMarket is equipped with a key constraint, a referential integrity constraint, and
a value constraint. The first invariant specifies that *stockId* is a key in the set of
stocks.

invariant
forall {Stock s1,s2 **in** stocks:
(s1.stockId()=s2.stockId()) **implies** s1.equals(s2) };

The second invariant specifies that *brokerId* is a key in the set of brokers:

invariant
forall {Broker b1,b2 **in** brokers:
(b1.brokerId()= b2.brokerId()) **implies** b1.equals(b2) };

The third invariant is a referential integrity constraint. It specifies that references
to the stock ids in each set of stocks of individual brokers actually exist in the set of
stocks:

invariant
forall {Broker b **in** brokers: **forall** {Stock sb **in** b.stocks():
   exists {Stock s **in** stocks: (sb.stockId() = s.stockId()) }
  };

The fourth invariant specifies that the price of all stocks is nonnegative:

invariant
forall {Stock s **in** stocks: s.price() > 0};

The schema *StockMarket* equipped with the above constraints is specified below:


```
class Stock {
  string stockId();
  float price();
  // public methods
}
class Broker {
  string brokerId();
  string name();
  Set<Stock> stocks();
  // public methods
}
class StockMarket: Schema {
[SpecPublic][Rep] private Set<Stock> stocks;
[SpecPublic][Rep] private Set<Broker> brokers;
invariant
forall {Stock s1,s2 in stocks:
  (s1.stockId()=s2.stockId()) implies s1.equals(s2) };
invariant
forall {Broker b1,b2 in brokers:
  (b1.brokerId()= b2.brokerId()) implies b1.equals(b2) };
invariant
forall {Broker b in brokers: forall {Stock sb in b.stocks():
    exists {Stock s in stocks: (sb.stockId() = s.stockId()) }
    };
// public methods for insertions, updates, and deletions of stocks and brokers
}
```

A schema is equipped with a collection of public methods, and the whole schema class is statically verified. A transaction can access the database only through schema methods. As an illustration, we specify a public method *deleteStock* because it involves maintaining the referential integrity constraint. The frame condition of this method expressed in the **modifies** clause specifies that the transaction affects only the set of stocks and the set of brokers. Violating this frame constraint will be detected by the Spec# compiler as a static error.

modifies stocks, brokers;

The precondition requires that a stock with the code of the stock *delStock* to be deleted does indeed exist in the set of stocks.

requires exists { Stock s **in** stocks:
    s.stockId()= delStock.stockId()};

There are several postconditions. The first one guarantees that the stock has been deleted from the set of stocks.

ensures forall { Stock s **in** stocks:
    s.stockId() != delStock.stockId()};

The second postcondition guarantees that the stocks that are different from the deleted stock have not been affected by this method, i.e., they are still in the set of stocks with the same price. The keyword **old** refers to the previous object state, i.e., the object state before method execution.

ensures forall {Stock s **in old**(stocks):
    s.stockId() != delStock.stockId() **implies**
    (Stock s **in** stocks()) ∧ (s.price()=**old**(s.price()))} ;

The third postcondition ensures that the brokers are unaffected by the delete method, i.e., all the brokers that existed before execution of this method are still in the set of stocks after execution of this method.

ensures forall {Broker b1 **in old**(brokers):
    exists { Broker b2 **in** brokers: (b2.brokerId()= b1.brokerId()) };

The fourth postcondition ensures that references to stocks of each broker actually exist in the set of stocks.

ensures
forall {Broker b **in** brokers:
    forall {Stock s **in** b.stocks():
    s.stockId() != delStock.stockId()}
    };

The last postcondition ensures that every broker that existed before method execution has a corresponding broker (that is, with the same id) after method execution with the same stocks except for the deleted stock.

ensures
forall {Broker b1 **in old**(brokers):
  exists unique {Broker b2 **in** brokers: (b2.brokerId()= b1.brokerId() ∧
    forall {Stock s **in** b1.stocks():
    s.stockId() != delStock.stockId() **implies**
    (s **in** b2.stocks()); }
  }
};

The method *deleteStock* with its frame constraint, precondition and postconditions is given below. The frame constraint is specified in the **modifies** clause. This clause specifies objects that this method is allowed to modify. An attempt to modify any other object will be detected as a compile-time error.

```
void deleteStock (Stock delStock) {
modifies stocks, brokers;
requires exists { Stock s in old(stocks):
    s.stockId()= delStock.stockId()};
ensures forall { Stock s in stocks:
    s.stockId() != delStock.stockId()};
ensures forall {Stock s in old(stocks):
  s.stockId() != delStock.stockId() implies
    (s in stocks()) ∧ (s.price()=old(s.price())} ;
ensures forall {Broker b1 in old(brokers):
  exists b2 in brokers: (b2.brokerId()= b1.brokerId()) };
ensures
forall {Broker b in brokers:
  forall {s in b.stocks():
  s.stockId() != delStock.stockId()}
ensures
forall {Broker b1 in old(brokers):
  exists unique {Broker b2 in brokers: (b2.brokerId()= b1.brokerId() ∧
    forall {Stock s in b1.stocks():
    s.stockId() != delStock.stockId() implies
    (s in b2.stocks()); }
  }
// code
};
```

A sample transaction *StockMerge* is specified below. This transaction performs a merge of two stocks s1 and s2 to create a new stock. The value of the new stock is computed by some rule from the values of the stocks to be merged. These two stocks are then deleted. This transaction is expressed as a composition of public methods associated with the class *StockMarket*.

The first two preconditions require that the stocks to be merged actually exist in the set of stocks.

requires exists unique {Stock s **in** stocks: s.stockId()=s1.stockId()};
requires exists unique {Stock s **in** stocks: s.stockId()=s2.stockId()};

The third postcondition ensures that there is a stock in the set of stocks after execution of the method *update* that did not exist in the set of stocks prior to execution of this method whose price is computed according to the rule specified in this method.

ensures exists unique {Stock s **in** stocks: !(s **in old**(stocks)) ∧
  (s.price()=(s1.price() + s2.price())/2 };

The fourth postcondition ensures that the merged stocks do not exist any more in the set of stocks.

ensures forall {Stock s **in** stocks:
(s.stockId() != s1.stockId()) ∧ (s.stockId() != s2.stockId()) };

The next postcondition ensures that stocks different from the merged stocks that existed in the set of stocks before execution of the method *update* are still in that set after execution of this method.

ensures forall {Stock s **in old**(stocks):
((s.stockId() != s1.stockId()) ∧ (s.stockId() != s2.stockId()
    implies s **in** stocks) };

The last postcondition ensures that the brokers and their stocks different from the merged stocks that existed before execution of the method *update* still exist after execution of this method.

ensures forall {Broker b1 **in old**(brokers):
  exists unique { Broker b2 **in** brokers:
    (b2.brokerId()= b1.brokerId()) ∧
    forall {Stock s **in** b1.stocks():
    ∧ s.stockId() != s1.stockId())∧
    s.stockId() != s2.stockId()
  implies s **in** b2.stocks; }
}

The transaction *StockMerge* with the above specified constraints is specified as follows:

class StockMerge: Transaction< StockMarket > {
void update(Stock s1,s2) {

modifies stocks, brokers;
requires exists unique {Stock s **in** stocks: s.stockId()=s1.stockId()}
requires exists unique {Stock s **in** stocks:
    s.stockId()=s2.stockId()}
ensures exists unique {Stock s **in** stocks: !(s **in old**(stocks)) ∧
  (s.price()=(s1.price() + s2.price())/2 }
ensures forall {Stock s **in** stocks:
(s.stockId() != s1.stockId()) ∧ (s.stockId() != s2.stockId()) }
ensures forall {Stock s **in old**(stocks):
((s.stockId() != s1.stockId()) ∧ (s.stockId() != s2.stockId()
    implies s **in** stocks) };
ensures forall {Broker b1 **in old**(brokers):
  exists unique {Broker b2 **in** brokers:
    (b2.brokerId()= b1.brokerId()) ∧
    forall {Stock s **in** b1.stocks():
    ∧ s.stockId() != s1.stockId())∧
    s.stockId() != s2.stockId()
  implies s **in** b2.stocks; };
  // code
  }
}

A simplified body of the transaction *StockMerge* is given below. A new stock is
created and initialized. Then its price is computed and updated based on the price of
the two stocks to be merged. Finally the two stocks that were merged are deleted.

```
{ Stock s3 = new Stock();
initializeStock(s3);
insertStock(s3);
updateStock(s3, s1.price() + s2.price())/2);
deleteStock(s1);
deleteStock(s2);
}
```

6.8 Exercises

1. Specify Code Contracts object invariants for the class *Portfolio* viewed as an
   aggregation of a collection of stocks and a collection of bonds.
2. Specify Code Contract object invariants of the class *Investor* in such a way that
   these assertions refer to the investor's portfolio.
3. Specify Code Contract object invariants of the class Registrar.
4. Specify Code contract object invariants of the class *Student*.
5. Specify Code Contracts assertions for the interface *IPortfolio*.
6. Specify Code Contracts assertions for the interface *InvestorI*.

7. Specify Code Contracts assertions for classes *Asset*, *Stock* and *Bond* in such a way that constraints for classes *Stock* and *Bond* are compatible with the constraints for class *Asset*.

8. Specify Code Contracts assertions for the class *Tournament* where a tournament is an aggregation of a collection of matches and a collection of players as in Fig. 6.9.

9. Specify Code Contracts assertions for the class *StockMarket*.

10. Specify Code Contracts assertions for the method *deleteStock* of the *StockMarket* schema.

11. Specify Code Contracts assertions for the method *mergeStocks* of the schema *StockMarket*.

Bibliographical Remarks

UML

UML website [17] contains various specification documents for UML. A software engineering textbook that is heavily based on UML is [7].

OCL

OCL specification documents are at the OMG (Object Management Group) website for OCL [15].

Assertion languages

Three major object-oriented assertion languages that are tied to particular object-oriented programming languages are Code Contracts [8], Java Modeling Language (not covered in this book) [16], and Spec # [14]. All of these languages implement a behavioral compatibility rules establish in [13].

Object-oriented programming languages

The basics of the technology of object-oriented programming languages and systems presented in this book are based on Java [4] and C# [1].

Software Engineering textbooks

Among many books on Software Engineering we mention [7] and [6]. The first one is informal, heavily based on UML and documentation. The second one is much more formal. Neither book covers software technologies that are covered in this book.

Data management

We presented two persistent technologies. The first one is Java Data Objects (JDO) which is object-oriented [9]. The second one is Java Persistence API [10], which is object-relational. A general model of orthogonal persistence is presented

© Springer International Publishing AG 2017   171
S. Alagić, *Software Engineering: Specification, Implementation, Verification,*
DOI 10.1007/978-3-319-61518-9

in [5]. Java model of persistence is explained in [4]. Query languages are presented using LINQ (Language Integrated Queries) [11].

Object-oriented technology

Various aspects of the object-oriented technology such as type systems, assertion languages, reflection, concurrent object-oriented programming, virtual platform, object databases and transactions are presented in a related book [2].

Verification techniques

Code Contracts is specified at its web site [8]. Specification and verification techniques using Code Contracts [8] are presented in [2]. Specification and verification techniques using Spec# are described in [12] and [2]. A complex application of these techniques as they apply to transaction verification is presented in [3].

References

1. J. Alabahari, B. Albahari, *C# 5.0 in a Nutshell* (O' Reilly, Sebastopol, CA, 2012)
2. S. Alagić, *Object-Oriented Technology* (Springer, Berlin, 2015)
3. S. Alagić, A. Fazeli, Verifiable object-oriented transactions, in *Proceedings of COB 2012 (Concurrent Objects and Beyond)*. Lecture Notes in Computer Science, vol. 8665 (2014), pp. 251–275
4. K. Arnold, J. Gosling, D. Holmes, *The Java Programming Language* (Addison-Wesley, Reading, 2000)
5. M. Atkinson, R. Morrison, Orthogonally persistent object systems. VLDB J. **4**, 319–401 (1995)
6. D. Bjorner, *Software Engineering* (Springer, Berlin, 2008)
7. B. Bruegge, A.H. Dutoit, *Object-Oriented Software Engineering* (Prentice Hall, Englewood Cliffs, 2010)
8. Code Contracts, Microsoft Research, https://msdn.microsoft.com/en-us/library/dd264808(v=vs.110).aspx
9. Java Data Objects (JDO), Apache, http://db.apache.org/jdo/
10. Java Persistence API, http://www.oracle.com/technetwork/java/javaee/tech/persistence-jsp-140049.html
11. Language Integrated Query, Microsoft Corporation, http://msdn.microsoft.com/en-us/vbasic/aa904594.aspx
12. K.R. Leino, P. Muller, Using Spec# language, methodology, and tools to write bug-free programs, Microsoft Research, http://research.microsoft.com/en-us/projects/specsharp/, 2010
13. B. Liskov, J.M. Wing, A behavioral notion of subtyping. ACM Trans. Program. Lang. Syst. **16**, 1811–1841 (1994)
14. Microsoft Corp., Spec#, http://research.microsoft.com/specsharp/
15. Object Constraint Language (OCL), http://www.omg.org/spec/OCL/2.4/
16. Open JML, http://sourceforge.net/apps/trac/jmlspecs/wiki/OpenJml
17. Unified Modelling Language (UML), http://www.omg.org/spec/UML/

Index

Printed in the United States
By Bookmasters